The Armchair Traveller Series

DON FERNANDO
W. SOMERSET MAUGHAM

BOOKS BY
W. SOMERSET MAUGHAM

THE GENTLEMAN IN THE PARLOUR
ASHENDEN: OR THE BRITISH AGENT
THE CASUARINA TREE
THE PAINTED VEIL
ON A CHINESE SCREEN
OF HUMAN BONDAGE
THE MOON AND SIXPENCE
THE TREMBLING OF A LEAF
LISA OF LAMBETH
MRS. CRADDOCK
THE EXPLORER
THE MAGICIAN
THE MERRY-GO-ROUND
THE LAND OF THE BLESSED VIRGIN
(SKETCHES AND IMPRESSIONS IN ANDALUSIA)

Plays

THE SACRED FLAME
THE LETTER
THE CONSTANT WIFE
THE CIRCLE
THE EXPLORER
MRS. DOT
A MAN OF HONOUR
PENELOPE
JACK STRAW
LADY FREDERICK
THE TENTH MAN
LANDED GENTRY
THE UNKNOWN
SMITH

DON FERNANDO

Or

VARIATIONS
ON SOME SPANISH THEMES

By

W. SOMERSET MAUGHAM

PARAGON HOUSE
NEW YORK

First paperback edition, 1990

Published in the United States by

Paragon House Publishers
90 Fifth Avenue
New York, NY 10011

Library of Congress Cataloging-in-Publication Data

Maugham, W. Somerset (William Somerset), 1874–1965.
Don Fernando, or, Variations on some Spanish themes /
by W. Somerset Maugham. — 1st pbk. ed.
p. cm. — (Armchair traveller series)
Reprint. Originally published: Garden City, N.Y. :
Doubleday, Doran, 1935.
ISBN 1-55778-269-5 : $9.95
1. Spain—Civilization—1516-1700. 2. Spanish
literature—Classical period, 1500-1700—History and
criticism. 3. Spain—Description and travel—1981-
I. Title. II. Title: Variations on some Spanish themes.
III. Series.
DP171.5.M39 1990
946—dc20 89-71112 CIP

This book is printed on acid-free paper
Manufactured in the United States of America
10 9 8 7 6 5 4 3 2

DON FERNANDO
W. SOMERSET MAUGHAM

I

I WAS living in Seville at the time, in the street
called Guzman el Bueno, and whenever I went out
or came home I passed Don Fernando's tavern.
When, my morning's work done, I had gone for a stroll
down the gay and crowded Sierpes, I found it very
pleasant to drop in for a glass of manzanilla on my way
back to luncheon; and in the cool of the evening,
walking my horse over the dangerous cobbles after a
ride in the country, I would often stop, call the boy
to hold the horse, and step in. The tavern was no more
than a long low room with doors on two sides of it,
for it was at the corner of a street; the bar ran down
the length of the room and behind it were the barrels
of wine from which Don Fernando served you. From
the ceiling hung bunches of Spanish onions, strings of
sausages and hams from Granada, which Don Fernando
always said were the best in Spain. I think his custom
was chiefly among the servants of the neighbourhood.
This district of Santa Cruz was then the most elegant
in Seville. Tortuous white streets, with large houses,

and here and there a church. It was strangely deserted. If you went out in the morning you might see a lady in black, with her maid, going to mass; sometimes a huckster passed along with his donkey, his wares in great open panniers; or a beggar, stopping at house after house, who raised his voice at each reja, the wrought iron gate that led into the patio, and begged for alms with the phrase of immemorial usage. At nightfall the ladies who had been driving in the Paseo in a landau drawn by two horses came home again and the streets resounded with the clatter of the horses' hooves. Then all again grew silent. This was many years ago. I write now of the last years of the nineteenth century.

Don Fernando was small even for a Spaniard, but he was very fat. His round brown face shone with sweat and he had always two days' growth of beard. Never more and never less. I do not know how he managed it. He was incredibly dirty. He had large black shining eyes, with extremely long lashes, and they were at the same time sharp, good-natured and gay. He was a wag and he enjoyed his own dry humour. He spoke in the soft Andalusian Spanish from which the Moorish influence has eliminated the harshness of Castile and it was not till I had learnt the language pretty well that I found him easy to understand. He was an aficionado of the bull-ring and it was his boast that the great Guerrita came in now and then to drink a glass of wine with him. He was a bachelor and lived alone with a scrubby, pale-faced boy whom he had got from the orphanage and who did the cooking, washed the glasses and swept the floor. This boy had the most pronounced squint I ever saw.

But Don Fernando did not only sell you as good a glass of manzanilla as you could get in Seville; he also dealt in curios. That was why I dropped in to see him so often. You never knew what he might have to show you. I suppose the things came through a confidential servant from the houses in the neighbourhood. Their owners, temporarily embarrassed, were too proud to take them to a shop. They were for the most part small and easily portable, pieces of silver, lace, old fans with sticks of mother-of-pearl decorated with gold, cruci-fixes, paste ornaments and antique rings of baroque design. Don Fernando seldom acquired a piece of furniture; but when he did, a bargueño or a pair of straight-backed chairs, with leather seats and all studded with nails, he would keep it upstairs in the bedroom he shared with the foundling. I had very little money and he knew I could only buy trifles, but he loved to show his purchases and two or three times he took me up into his room. The windows were closed to keep out the heat by day and the noxious airs by night and it was very dirty. It stank. In opposite corners of the room were two small iron beds, unmade at whatever time of day you went in, and the sheets looked as though they had not been washed for months. The floor was strewn with cigarette-ends. Don Fernando's eyes would shine more brightly than ever when he passed his grubby, podgy hand over the wood of a chair that had been polished by the usage of three centuries. He would spit on the dusty gilt surface of a tabernacle and rub the place with his finger to show you with delight the exquisite quality of the gold. Sometimes, while you stood at the bar, he would fish out from behind it the pieces of a pair of ear-rings, those old heavy Spanish ear-rings in three tiers, and assemble them delicately so that you might admire the beauty of the paste and the elegance of the setting. He had a way of handling these things, sensual and tender, that showed you more than any words he might have spoken how profound a feeling he had for them. When he flicked open an old fan, with the peculiar click that the Spanish woman gives, and fanned himself, an old fan a great lady in her mantilla had flaunted at a bull-fight when Charles III was King of Spain, you could not but feel that, ignorant though he was, he had some vague, delightful emotion of the past.

Don Fernando bought cheaply and sold cheaply; and so, after bargaining for days, often for weeks, which I think we both enjoyed, I was able to get from him little by little a number of objects which were not of the smallest use to me, but which I hankered after because their associations appealed to my fancy. So I bought the fans that pretty women, dead a hundred and fifty years ago, had flirted, the ear-rings they wore in their ears, the fantastic rings they wore on their fingers and the crucifixes they hung in their rooms. It was junk and in the passage of time it has all been stolen, lost or given away. Of all I bought from Don Fernando I have now nothing but a book, and that I did not want and bought against my will. One day as I stepped across the threshold Don Fernando addressed me forthwith.

'I've got something for you,' he said. 'I bought it especially for you.'

'What is it?'

'A book.'

He opened a drawer in the bar and brought out a little squat volume bound in dirty parchment. My face fell.

'I don't want that.'

'But look at it. It's an old book. It's more than three hundred years old.'

He opened it and showed me the title page. There it was all right, the date 1586, with the imprint of Madrid and the publisher's name: Por la viuda de Alonso Gomez Impressor de la C.R.M.

'It doesn't cost anything,' he went on. 'I'll give it you for fifty pesetas.'

'But I don't want it at any price.'

'It's a celebrated book. When it was brought to me I said to myself: Don Guillermo will like that. He's an educated man.'

'My eye and Betty Martin.' (Not many people know the Spanish for that.) 'Sell it to somebody else. I'm not a book collector. I only buy books to read.'

'But why shouldn't you read this? It's very interesting.'

'Not to me.'

'A book three hundred years old? Come, man, don't say things like that to me. Look, there's writing on the margins in places and there's writing on the back page. That shows you it's old.'

It was true that some reader had written notes here and there in a hand that might very well have been of the seventeenth century, but I could not decipher a word. I turned a few pages. It was beautifully printed on strong, fine paper, but the type was so close-set that it was difficult to read. The old spelling, the abbreviations I noticed, made it hard to understand. I shook my head firmly and handed the book back to Don Fernando.

'You can have it for forty pesetas. I paid thirty-five for it myself.'

'I wouldn't have it as a gift.'

He shrugged his shoulders with a sigh and put the book away.

A few days later I happened to pass the tavern on horseback and Don Fernando, who was standing at the doorway sucking a toothpick, called me.

'Come in a moment; I've got something to say to you.'

I dismounted and gave the bridle to the boy. Don Fernando put the book in my hands.

'I'll give it you for thirty pesetas. I lose five on it, but I want you to have it.'

'But I don't want the book,' I cried.

'Twenty-five pesetas.'

'No.'

'You needn't read it. Put it in your library.'

'I haven't got a library.'

'But you ought to have a library. Start your library with this book. It's a beautiful book.'

'It isn't a beautiful book.'

And it wasn't. Even though I knew I should never read it I might have been tempted if it had been bound in leather with a coat of arms in gold, a handsome folio with wide margins. But it was an ugly little volume, much too thick for its height, and the parchment with which it was bound was crinkled and yellow. I was determined not to have the book. Don Fernando, I do not know why, was determined that I should; and after that I never went into the tavern without his attacking me. He flattered me, he cajoled me, he threw himself on my mercy, he appealed to my sense of justice; he came down in his price to twenty pesetas, to ten, but I stood firm. Then one day he got hold of a wooden statuette of St. Anthony, obviously of the seventeenth century, beautifully carved and painted, that I immediately set my heart on. We bargained over it for several weeks until at last we arrived somewhere near the price that he was prepared to let it go for and that I was able to pay. The difference between us was only twenty pesetas. I forget the exact sum. I think he was asking a hundred and thirty pesetas and I was offering a hundred and ten.

'Give me a hundred and thirty for the statue and the book,' he said, 'and you'll never regret it.'

'Curse the book,' I cried in exasperation.

I paid for my drink and walked to the door. Don Fernando called me back.

'Listen,' he said.

I turned round. He came towards me, an ingratiating smile on his fat, red lips, with the statuette in one hand and the book in the other.

'I'll give you the statuette for a hundred and twenty pesetas and I'll make you a present of the book.'

A hundred and twenty pesetas was the price I had all along made up my mind to give.

'I'll pay that,' I said, 'but you can keep the book.'

'It's a present.'

'I don't want a present.'

'But I want to make you one. It's a pleasure for me. You can't refuse a present. Come, man.'

I sighed. I was beaten. I was a trifle ashamed.

'I'll give you twenty pesetas for the book.'

'Even at that it's a present,' he said. 'You could sell it in Madrid for two hundred.'

He wrapped it up in a dirty piece of newspaper; I paid my money, and with the book in my hand and the statuette under my arm, walked home.

II

IN course of time I gathered together something of
a library and the little squat book that Don Fernando
forced upon me found its place in it. Because of its
shape and its parchment binding among the paper
covers of my foreign books and the multicoloured cloth
of the English ones it often caught my eye. It did not
irritate me for it reminded me of Don Fernando's
tavern, the streets of Seville in summer (the glare miti-
gated by the awnings stretched across them), and the
cool, dry taste of manzanilla; but I never thought of
reading it. And then one rainy afternoon when I was
browsing among my books I happened to notice it
and took it from the shelf. I turned over a few pages
idly. I thought I would read a paragraph and see what
I could make of it. But the paragraph was six pages
long. I did not find it so hard to understand as I had
expected. The long s's were a bit of a bother and the
n's, omitted according to no obvious plan, were indicated by a little squiggle on the preceding letter; v in
the middle of a word was replaced by u, and at the
beginning sometimes by b. This reproduced the pro-
nunciation of the sixteenth century. But, unfamiliar

with this as I was, it was something of a facer when I had to guess that the word spelt boluer must be read volver. There were many abbreviations and the spelling was archaic. But I found that if I read with attention there was no great difficulty to overcome and the author seemed to me to write with perspicacity. He said what he had to say briefly. I turned back and started at the beginning.

The story I read was strange. Its hero was the youngest son of the thirteen children of a certain Don Beltran Yañez de Oñaz and of his wife Doña Maria Saez de Balda. Don Beltran was the head of an ancient and illustrious house, and his wife was his equal in birth and virtue. They were related to the greatest families in the province of Guipuzcoa. This is one of the pleasantest parts of Spain, a hilly country, with green, fertile valleys through which run bubbling crystalline streams. The cold in winter is tolerable and in summer the air is cool and fresh. Don Beltran's house stands in a long, narrow valley closed in by hills in front and by hills behind. But the view, though thus confined, is spacious. The summits of the hills are bare and stony, but trees grow on the sides, and on the lower slopes are patches of pasture, maize and corn. It is a smiling, richly coloured scene. A little river runs through the valley and it may be supposed that it was for the convenience of this that the house was built at that spot. But the times were troublous, and though no longer the fortress that had been destroyed by order of King Henry the Fourth and the Brotherhoods of Guipuzcoa, it could be defended in case of need. It is a square building, the lower part (the remains of the fourteenth century stronghold) of grey untrimmed stone, but the upper part, built a century later in a less warlike manner, is of brick, with little pepper-pot towers called bartizans decorating the four corners. It is not very large; in England it would seem a country house of but moderate size, and Don Beltran and his wife, with their large family and the number of servants that their station demanded, must have been somewhat crowded. Don Beltran was a man of consequence and his heir, Don Martin, married Doña Magdalena d'Araoz, maid of honour to Queen Isabella the Catholic, who gave her as a wedding-present a painting of the Annunciation. A few days after the bride arrived in her new home she was surprised to find the picture bathed in sweat. The miracle caused great surprise to all the members of the family and Don Pedro Lopez, her husband's brother and a priest, proposed that the picture should be transferred to the village church for the veneration of the faithful. But Don Martin, unwilling to part with so great a treasure, offered instead to build a chapel in the house, where the miraculous painting might be suitably enshrined.

The youngest son of Don Beltran, the hero of the story I read, was christened Iñigo. When little more than

a child he was sent by his father to Court and here
entered the service of Don Juan Velazquez de Cuellar,
treasurer to the Catholic Kings. Service was an
honourable calling. Men of rank thought it no disgrace
to place their sons in the households of great noblemen.
They waited at table, made the beds, lit the fires, swept
the floors and fetched and carried for their masters.
Don Juan Velazquez was governor of Arevalo in the
province of Avila, one of the cities left by Juan II of
Castile to his widow, the mother of Isabella. The arms
of Arevalo show a battlemented wall and a plumed
knight in full armour on horseback, with his lance at
rest. Here the young Iñigo learnt manners, the usages
of the world and such accomplishments as became a
gentleman. Growing to man's estate, with the example
before him of his brothers, who were goodly men, and
urged by his own gallant spirit, he applied himself to
the exercise of arms. He sought to excel his equals and
to achieve a reputation for valour. But his biographer
passes over this period of his life briefly. It is only from
his own casual remarks made in after life that he is
known to have been quick to defend his honour when
the occasion arose, to have loved the chase and to have
been something of a gambler. He was a young man of
a comely person, not very tall, but well-made, with
small feet of which he was not a little proud; he admitted
in later years that he liked to wear boots that were
too tight for him. He had beautiful hair, of a chestnut

colour with a reddish glint in it, and his brown eyes were large, moving and wonderfully eloquent. His skin was white. His nose was hooked; it was the most noticeable feature of his face, but it was not so large as to be a disfigurement. He wore with grace the rich clothes of the court. For the sober habit which the economical spirit of Ferdinand the Catholic had except on occasions of state made usual, gave way with the arrival of Philip the Handsome, and his Flemish followers, to fashions of great extravagance. Don Iñigo was of an amorous complexion and is reputed to have been the lover of Germaine de Foix, the young wife whom Ferdinand, notwithstanding his name of the Prudent, married after the death of Isabella. The French chronicler describes her as 'bonne et fort belle princesse,' but another contemporary, a Spaniard, states that she was ill-favoured and lame. He was possibly prejudiced. 'This lady introduced into Castile magnificent dinners, albeit the Castilians and even their kings are very moderate in this matter,' he says severely. 'Whoever spent money on parties and banquets for her was her friend.' She was but eighteen when she married (Ferdinand being fifty-four) and it is not strange if she liked to amuse herself. Don Iñigo fell passionately in love with her. He wore her colours and composed madrigals in her honour. He was a very proper gentleman.

He lived a life of ease and gallantry till the age of twenty-seven when, King Ferdinand being dead and

his widow remarried, he entered the service of Don
Antonio Manrique, Duke of Najera, a patron of his
house. He took part in various campaigns. He was
ambitious and energetic. He had a native gift for the
managing of men so that the Duke of Najera employed
him in affairs that needed discretion. On one occasion
he sent him on a mission to reconcile contending factions
in Guipuzcoa, and Don Iñigo succeeded in settling the
matters in dispute to the satisfaction of all concerned.
Charles V began his reign over Spain with a series of
mistakes that drove his new subjects to revolt. The
King of France seized the opportunity to declare war
on his rival and a French army entered Navarre. The
Duke of Najera, who was in command of the Spanish
troops, leaving a garrison in the city of Pampeluna,
evacuated the country. The French laid siege to the
city, and the officers of the garrison, among whom was
Don Iñigo, seeing no help for it, were of a mind to
capitulate; but Don Iñigo opposed the common judgement and by his eloquence filled them with his own
spirit so that they determined to resist to the death.
But in the course of the assault he was hit by a cannon-
ball in the right leg, and a splinter of stone from the
wall at the same time wounded his other leg also. He
fell and the garrison who had been sustained by his
courage lost heart and surrendered.

The French entered the city. When they came upon
Don Iñigo and discovered who he was they were moved

to compassion and tended his wounds. So that he might be better taken care of, the French commander with generous courtesy gave orders that as soon as it was possible he should be borne back to his own house in a litter. But no sooner was he there than his wounds, especially that on his right leg, grew worse. The surgeons formed the opinion that in order to set it properly the bone must be broken again. This was done, to the great pain of the sick man, but during the operation he neither changed colour, groaned nor said a word that discovered want of courage. He did not mend, however, and little hope remained that he would recover. He was told of his danger, whereupon he confessed and received the sacrament of extreme unction. But that night, St. Peter, for whom he had always had a devotion, appeared to him and restored him to health. His bones began to set and he grew stronger. Twenty splinters of bone had been removed from his leg, so that it was shorter than the other and mis-shapen; and he could neither walk nor stand. Below the knee a piece of bone protruded in an unsightly manner and this distressed him so much that he asked the surgeons how it might be remedied. They told him that the excrescence could be cut away, but it would cause him greater anguish than he had ever endured in his life. His intention was to proceed with the career of arms; he was vain, he wanted to wear the smart boots that were then in fashion; and so notwithstanding their hesitation he insisted that the operation should be performed. He would not consent to be tied down, thinking this unworthy of his generous soul, and bore the suffering without a movement and without a murmur. The deformity was removed and then by means of wheels and other instruments, which caused him horrible pain, they gradually stretched and straightened the leg. But it never attained the same length as the other and he limped to the end of his life.

To pass the tedious hours of his convalescence he asked for the novels of chivalry which he was fond of reading, but it happened that there were none in the house. They gave him what books they had, and these were a life of Christ and the stories of the saints which were known as Flos Sanctorum. He began to read, carelessly enough, but in a little while was deeply moved, and presently there arose in him a desire to imitate the great deeds of which he read. But he could not at once forget the past and he was beset by memories of his warlike exploits, the pleasant occupations of the court and thoughts of love. God and the Devil contended for his soul. But he noticed that when he thought of things divine he was filled with exultation, and contrariwise when he thought of things of the world, with discontent. That was enough. He determined to alter his life. His bitterest torment was the love that he sought in vain to tear out of his yearning heart; and one night, when he rose from his bed to pray, as was his frequent habit, the Queen of Heaven, with the child in her arms, appeared to him. From that time he was freed from the sensual thoughts that had vexed him, so that to the end of his life he preserved the chastity of his soul without stain.

His elder brother, and the people of the house, saw that he was different, for though he kept his secret his manner was changed. They must indeed have guessed that something very odd was going on, for when the young soldier finally made up his mind to follow in the footsteps of Jesus the house was rocked with a great crash and the stout stone wall was split through its entire thickness. It was observed that he read a great deal (an occupation naturally unfitting for a man of his birth) and prayed, and no longer cared to jest; his speech was grave and measured, of spiritual things, and he wrote much. He had a book elegantly bound and in this, for he was a good scribe, wrote down the most remarkable sayings and deeds of Jesus, of Mary, and of the Saints. He wrote those of Jesus in letters of gold, those of his blessed mother in letters of blue, and those of the other saints in other colours according to his devotion to them. He found satisfaction in these pursuits, but in none greater than in the contemplation of the sky and the stars. It stimulated him to contempt of all mutable things which are beneath them and enflamed his love of God. This habit never left him and his biographer relates how in old age when he could behold the heavens from some height he would remain absorbed in the sight so that he seemed transported. When he returned to himself the tears poured from his eyes with the delight that filled his heart and he said: 'how vile and base appears the earth when I look at the sky; it is but mud and dung.' He resolved to go to Jerusalem as soon as he had recovered his health. Till this was possible he decided with fasting, penitences of various kinds and corporal punishment to persecute his flesh. He sought a manner of life in which, stamping earthly things and the vanities of the world beneath his feet, he might castigate himself with such rigour as to give satisfaction to his Redeemer.

When at last he was sufficiently well to set out on his pilgrimage, Don Iñigo, knowing that it would arouse opposition in his family, gave as a pretext for leaving the house his desire to visit his protector, the Duke of Najera, who had sent several times during his illness to enquire after him. But his elder brother, Don Martin, suspecting that the journey he was taking had another motive than civility, called him aside.

'All things are great in you, my brother,' he said, 'your intelligence, your judgement, your courage, your birth, your appearance, your influence with the great, the goodwill in which this country holds you, the use and experience of war, sense and prudence, your age which is now in the flower of youth, and the great expectations, founded on these facts, which all men have of you. So how can you for a whim, deceiving our well-founded hopes, make fools of us all, and dispossess our house of the trophies of your victories and of the profits and rewards that should ensue from your labours? I have one advantage only over you, that I was born before you; but in everything else I recognise that you excel me. Look, I beg you, brother dearer than my life, look what you do and adopt not a course that will not only cheat us of our hopes, but will also cast upon our lineage perpetual infamy and disgrace.'

Don Iñigo answered in few words. He said that he would not forget that he was well-born, and he promised to do nothing to bring dishonour on his house. He set out accompanied by two servants, but, giving them presents, soon afterwards dismissed them. His immediate destination was Monserrat. From the day he left his father's house he scourged himself every night. He desired to do great and difficult things and he mortified his body with severity, because the saints, whose example he sought to follow, had thus acquitted themselves. In this he aimed, not so much at atoning for his sins, as at pleasing God. The road led over hill and dale, sometimes along a rivulet, sometimes high above; a pleasant, green and smiling country. From the top of a hill the hills all round looked like a great flock of sheep; and on the banks of the stream trees grew thickly, oaks and chestnuts, acacias, beech and

poplar. At a certain place Don Iñigo was overtaken by
a Moor, of whom at that time there were still many in
the kingdoms of Valencia and Aragon, and they rode
for a space together. They began to talk and presently
discussed the virginity of Our Lady. The Moor admitted that she had enjoyed this blessed state before
and at the birth of Jesus, but denied that she had
retained it afterwards. Don Iñigo did all he could to
undeceive him, but, such was his knavishness, he would
not listen to reason. The Moor rode on, leaving Don
Iñigo much perplexed; he could not decide whether his
faith, and Christian charity, did not demand that he
should pursue the fellow and stab him to the death for
his audacity. He was a soldier, punctilious in the point
of honour, and he took it as a personal affront that an
enemy of the faith should venture in his presence to
speak with disrespect of the Queen of Heaven. After
anxious consideration he decided to leave the matter
to the arbitrament of God; he made up his mind to
go on his way till he came to a cross-road and there
drop the reins on his horse's neck. If the horse took
the road along which the Moor had gone he would
follow and kill him. But if the horse took the other
road he would let him be. Thus he did and the horse,
leaving on one side the broad and flat road along which
the Moor had ridden, chose the other. God had spoken.
Arriving at length in the neighbourhood of Monserrat
Don Iñigo reached a village where he provided himself

with what little he needed for his pilgrimage. He bought a tunic of rough coarse stuff that reached to his feet, a piece of rope for a belt, espadrilles, a staff and a drinking-vessel.

Monserrat was a Benedictine monastery famous for the miracles that were constantly worked there and for the great concourse of people that came from all parts to ask favours of the Holy Virgin. Don Iñigo on his arrival sought out a confessor. He made a general confession that lasted three days. He then gave his horse to the monastery, and laid his sword and his dagger before the altar of Our Lady. When the night came he went to a poor man and giving him all his clothes, even his shirt, dressed himself in the coarse habit he had bought. And because he had read in the books of chivalry that it was the custom of new-made knights to keep vigil over their arms, Don Iñigo, the new-made knight of Christ, spent the night watching before the image of the Blessed Virgin, and bitterly weeping for his sins resolved to amend his life from then on. Before dawn, so that none should know whither he went, he abandoned the high road that led to Barcelona (whence it would have been natural to take ship for Italy) and with all speed started for a village in the mountains called Manresa. He wore his pilgrim clothes, but since his wound still troubled him he had one foot shod. But he had not gone a league before he found that a man was following him and calling. The man asked him if it was true that he had given his rich clothes to a beggar. For, finding him with them and thinking he had stolen them, they had cast the fellow into prison. Don Iñigo confessed that he had indeed given him the clothes, but when the man asked him who he was and whence he came he would not answer.

At Manresa, concealing his birth and the manner of his life aforetime, he took up his abode in the hospital of the poor; and because in the world he had been careful of his person and vain of his beautiful hair, which he had been accustomed to wear long, now he neglected it and went barehead. He allowed his beard and nails to grow. Every day he scourged himself three times and spent seven hours on his knees. Every day he went to mass, to vespers and to compline. Every day he begged for alms. But he neither ate meat nor drank wine; he lived on bread and water. He slept on the ground, passing the greater part of the night in prayer. He was careful to deny himself everything that could be of pleasure to his body, and though he was a robust man and a strong one in a little while the severity of his mortifications reduced him to very great weakness. But one day in the hospital with that beggarly crew, amid squalor and filth, he asked himself: 'What are you doing in this stench and vileness? Why do you go dressed so poorly and in so disgraceful a fashion? Do you not see that by consorting with people so base, and behaving like one of them, you obscure the greatness of your lineage?' He knew it was the voice of the devil and drew nearer still to the poor people and constrained himself to use them in a more friendly way. Another day, worn out and tired, the thought came to him that it was impossible for him to endure, for seventy years it might be, a life worse than a savage's, so harsh and wretched. 'And what,' he answered, 'are seventy years of penitence compared with eternity?' After a time the peace of soul that had been his comfort deserted him and he felt a great dryness in his heart; his spirit seemed constricted and he prayed without satisfaction or relief. He was seized with scruples that in his general confession he had not said all that he should have said. His conscience smote him so that, tortured with anxiety, he passed his nights in bitter tears. On one occasion, when he had left the hospital and was living in a Dominican monastery, his despair was such that he was tempted to throw himself out of the window of his cell. It was then that it profited him to have read the Flos Sanctorum, for he remembered the example of a saint who, wanting something from God, decided to fast till it was vouchsafed him; and in imitation Don Iñigo made up his mind neither to eat nor drink till he secured the peace of mind he desired. Nothing passed his lips for a week, during which time he continued to pray for seven hours a day on his knees, scourged himself thrice daily and performed the other devotions that he was used to. At the end of it he found himself strong enough to continue, but his confessor ordered him to eat and refused to give him absolution till he did. He broke his fast and in a short while was completely delivered of his scruples; he buried the memory of his past sins and was never more troubled by them.

Further mercies were then vouchsafed to the penitent. One day, being in prayer on the steps of the church of St. Dominic, his spirit was lifted up and he saw, as with his eyes, the form of the Holy Trinity. The vision filled him with such great comfort that he could neither think nor speak of anything else. He expounded the mystery with such an abundance of reasons, similes and examples, that all who heard him were overcome with admiration and surprise. Often, while praying, he perceived the Sacred Humanity of Jesus Christ and sometimes also the glorious and blessed Virgin Mary. One day, walking a little way out of Manresa, occupied with the contemplation of divine things, he sat down by the side of a stream and gazed at the flowing water; on a sudden his eyes were opened and he saw (not sensibly, but after a higher and more immaterial manner), with a new and unaccustomed light, so that he understood not only the mysteries of the faith, but also the mysteries of all knowledge. He affirmed at the end of his life that none of the knowledge that he had afterwards acquired either by study or by supernatural grace had the fullness of the knowledge he received in that moment of illumination.

One Saturday, occupied as usual with his devotional

exercises, he fell into a swoon, and those about him thought he was dead and would have buried him if one, feeling his pulse, had not observed that his heart still beat. He remained in this condition till the following Saturday when he awoke as from a sweet sleep.

Exhausted by excessive labours of the body and incessant combats of the soul he found himself constrained to rest a little; but visions so wonderful came to him and consolations so sweet, he was unable to give to sleep even the short time he had assigned to it and passed his nights in transport. He fell so seriously ill that his life was despaired of. As he prepared himself for death Satan suggested to him the notion that being a just and pious man he need not fear. It terrified him and with all his might he fought against it, trying by the recollection of his past sins to wrench out of his heart the devilish hope in the mercy of God; and when he was well enough to speak he begged those who were present when they saw him in the agony of death with great care to say to him: 'O miserable sinner, O luckless man, remember the evil thou hast done and the offences with which thou hast called down on thee the anger of God.' Having somewhat recovered he immediately resumed his accustomed penances and his austere mode of life. Striving with indefatigable determination to conquer himself, he laid upon his weary body burdens greater than it could bear and he fell gravely ill a second and a third time. At last experience, and a great pain in his stomach, combined with the rigour of the weather, for it was winter, persuaded him at least to clothe himself sufficiently to keep out the cold. In this manner he lived for the greater part of a year and then the time arrived when he was ready to start on his pilgrimage to Jerusalem. There were some who offered to bear him company and others who advised him not to attempt so long and arduous a journey without someone who knew Italian or Latin to serve as a guide and interpreter. But he desired to be alone with God so that he might enjoy communion with him without let or hindrance. He placed his confidence in Him and he was unwilling to betray it by relying on the assistance of another. He set out for Barcelona and his distant goal with no other company than God's.

Such was the early life of Don Iñigo de Oñaz, a Spanish gentleman, known to history as Saint Ignatius Loyola. The reader will long since have guessed it, for the tale I have told is well-known. The book that Don Fernando made me, all unwilling, buy was the life that was written of him not long after his death by Father Pedro de Ribadeneyra of the Company of Jesus.

III

I HAD long known Pampeluna. It stands on a height and is surrounded by low hills. They are pale under the blue sky. Their sides are cultivated and here and there are patches of maize, then patches of dry earth where the wheat has been gathered; but it must need incessant labour for the peasant to wring from that stony soil his difficult living. There are few trees in the plain but poplars. There is a small wood where they stand, side by side, but a little scattered, with a sort of shy eagerness. They make you think of a group of slim seminarists gathered about the door of the lecture hall to applaud the doctor of divinity who has just won a notable victory for the faith.

Pampeluna is a provincial town of no great size and it has little to attract the visitor. The plaza de la Constituçion has been renamed plaza de la Republica. In the cafés that surround it, before an empty glass, under awnings, the inhabitants sit all day long. In the centre is a bandstand and here without doubt will one day have place the statue of the first president of the republic. The narrow, winding streets of the mediaeval city have been broadened and straightened and there are plate-glass windows in the shops. The houses have miradors in which hour after hour women sit, looking down on the street below, sewing and gossiping. Overhead is a spider's web of telegraph wires, telephone lines and electric light cables. No longer does each craft occupy its particular quarter, but on the rampart behind the cathedral you may still see the rope-makers making rope in the same way as they have for centuries, oiling their shuttles from oil in a cow's horn, and the makers of espadrilles sewing as though for dear life; which indeed they are.

From morning till late into the night there is a ceaseless din. The toot of motor-horns, the splutter of exhausts and the tinkling of bicycle-bells, the rumble of carts over cobbled stones, the braying of asses and the clatter of hooves, the playing of pianos and the harsh clamour of gramophones; and above all, a continuous accompaniment, the piercing sound of voices raised in animated conversation. At the spot where Ignatius received his wound they have built a chapel and next to it a church. In the chapel is a picture in which you see the saint, no saint then, lying on the ground while his companions attend to his wounded leg. A man on a white horse watches the scene with indifference, but above the wounded hero an angel hovers, a prey to agitation. In the background is the city's formidable wall. The church is uglier than any church I have ever seen. Its decorations remind you of those of the scent shops in the rue de la Paix. It is spick and span, and looks as though it had cost any amount of money. I cannot believe that religious art has ever sunk lower than this; and that an earthquake has not levelled it with the ground must seem to the good Catholic a very signal instance of the infinite patience of God. Large parts of the walls have been demolished for the expansion of the city, but such parts as remain are impressive. They were rebuilt, it appears, by Philip II and the city since then has proved itself impregnable. At their base a little river runs. It is bordered by a meadow in which trees grow, affording a grateful shade, and here groups of people, some on the bank fishing, others sitting down engaged in conversation, make a pleasant picture that reminds you of a painting by one of the French impressionists.

But I had never been to Loyola, Azpeitia or Manresa, all three closely associated with the founder of the Company of Jesus, and these after reading his life I made it my business to visit. It was at Azpeitia that Don Iñigo was baptized and in the church you are shown the font at which the ceremony was performed. It has been smartened up with wooden decorations and a carved top. On each side are stone fonts at which it was hoped later inhabitants of the neighbourhood would have their children christened, but they have continued to insist on using that which the saint had exalted. The sacristan tells you with indulgence that they hope thus to enable their offspring to partake of his sanctity. Loyola is less than a mile away and now a broad avenue of trees conducts you to it. As you drive up you come to a statue of Saint Ignatius. The fine portico of the basilica faces you. This is in the Jesuit style of the seventeenth century, somewhat highly decorated, and a flight of steps leads up to it. The interior has a massive nobility. On the left, enclosed in great stone buildings, is the ancestral house of the Loyolas. The exterior has kept its old appearance, but the rooms within have been converted into chapels; the walls are lined with marble and the windows are of coloured glass. An imposing flight of stairs has replaced the old one and the wooden balusters are in the flamboyant style of the eighties. On an upper floor you are shown the little room which Don Iñigo as a child shared with one of his brothers. Next door to it is a low, wide chamber, with great beams, in which he read and prayed during his convalescence. Here, on a gold settle, is a statue of him in his best clothes, with a cushion behind him and a book in his hand, in the very act of being converted. There is a marble altar at which the privileged may pray. It is very magnificent and extremely ugly.

After that I went to Manresa. It is pleasant to drive through that sunny country. The colour has not the pastel lightness of French landscape, but is deeper and richer. The sky is bright blue with small stationary clouds very white against it. The hills are covered with pine trees and in the sun their green is brilliant. Round the town they are more thinly grown with stunted olives. You accompany a swift little river bordered with bulrushes, poplars and beech trees, but passing through the town it grows placid, as though in that quiet place it were unseemly to hasten. It is spanned by a slim bridge, plain but very graceful, with a tall arch in the middle rising to a point; and on its banks the houses are huddled together, old tall houses with open loggias in which the washing is hung out to dry.

It was in Manresa that Saint Ignatius wrote the first draft of a little book that has had a prodigious influence. This is the Spiritual Exercises. The visitor is shown the cave in which the saint, according to tradition, composed it. It is on the side of a rocky hill and from it you have a splendid prospect of Monserrat, sharp-edged on a clear day, but in the mist incredibly mysterious. It is shallow, but long and high, rugged, and open to the view. It can never have been a place of extreme seclusion. Now it is guarded by an enormous iron grille and over it is built a Jesuit college and a church. But the Jesuits have been expelled and the buildings are barred and locked.

The book is one that cannot be read without awe. For it must be remembered that it was the efficacious instrument that enabled the Society of Jesus for centuries to maintain its ascendancy. Four hundred commentaries have been written on it; popes, cardinals and bishops have commended it. Leo XIII said of it: 'Here is the sustenance that I desired for my soul.' So remarkable did the exercises seem even to the saint's contemporaries, the saint being when he wrote ignorant and unlettered, that a supernatural origin was very generally ascribed to them; and this was substantiated by the Blessed Virgin herself who appeared to Doña Maria Escobar and in so many words told her that she had been the assistant and instructress of Saint Ignatius in their composition. The illustrious collaborators did not, for some reason, see fit to mention the fact that a Spanish monk Francisco Garcia de Cisneros, Abbot of Monserrat, had some years before published a similar work with a title that was almost identical; and in Ludolph's Life of Christ there are, it appears, so many points in common with the Spiritual Exercises that it seems impossible to acquit the authors of plagiarism. This has, to my mind unreasonably, disquieted a good many people. I look upon the offence with indulgence. We writers get our material from one source and another (je prends mon bien où je le trouve) and the fact is, we only acknowledge the debt when we cannot help ourselves. But I see no reason why the Blessed Virgin should not have dictated this interesting material to the Abbot of Monserrat and to Ludolph the Carthusian as well as to Saint Ignatius. Authors repeat themselves and when they have got hold of an idea that appeals to them are apt to harp upon it.

The title is impressive: 'Spiritual Exercises for overcoming oneself and for regulating one's life without being swayed by any inordinate attachment.' A noble aim! It must be a dull mind that is not curious to see what plan this strange man devised to effect so difficult a process. For, notwithstanding his borrowings, it is clear that this book is the fruit of his own experience. Every page bears the stamp of his ruthless personality.

The exercises are divided into four weeks, but each week may be of shorter or longer duration, and they are performed under the guidance of a director. The root of the matter is told you at once. 'Man was created to praise, revere and serve God our Lord, and thereby to save his soul. And the other things on the face of the earth were created for man's sake, and to help him in the attainment of the end for which he was created. Hence it follows that man should make use of creatures so far as they help him towards his end, and should withdraw from them so far as they are a hindrance to him in regard to that end. Wherefore it is necessary that we should acquire detachment from all created things (in all that is left to the liberty of our free will and is not forbidden it), so that we on our part should not wish for health rather than sickness, for wealth rather than poverty, for honour rather than shame, for a long life rather than a short one, and so in all other matters, solely desiring and choosing those things

34

that may better lead us to the end for which we were created.'

A number of precepts are given to enable the exercitant to acquire concentration and so achieve what he desires.

' . . . after going to bed, when I am composing myself to sleep, for the interval of one Hail Mary to think of the hour at which I should rise, and to what purpose, recapitulating the exercise that I have to make.

' . . . When I awake . . . immediately to advert to what I am about to contemplate in the first exercise at midnight, moving myself to confusion over those many sins of mine, proposing examples, as if some knight were being arraigned before his king and his full assembled Court, stricken with shame and confusion at having grievously offended him of whom he had hitherto received many gifts and many favours.'

Before the exercitant reaches the place where he is to make his meditation he is bidden to stand for the space of a Pater Noster, with mind uplifted; then he enters upon his meditation, 'now kneeling, now prostrate on the ground, now lying back with uplifted face, now sitting, now standing.' When it is finished he is to spend a quarter of an hour, sitting or walking, during which he must consider what success he has had in it. He is ordered to avoid thinking of agreeable subjects, since the feeling of grief for his sins is hindered by any

consideration of joy. He must deprive himself of all
bright light, closing shutters and doors, except when he
is praying, reading and eating. He is not to laugh or to
say anything to provoke laughter. He is enjoined to do
penance; interior penance, which is to grieve over his
sins, with the firm purpose of not committing them or
any others again; and exterior penance, which is
chastisement for sins committed. This is taken in three
ways. 'The first regards food: that is to say, when we
take away superfluities, it is not penance but temperance: penance is when we take away from what it is
fitting that we should have; and the more and more, the
greater and better the penance, provided the con-
stitution be not impaired nor notable infirmity ensue.
The second way regards our amount of sleep; and in
like manner it is not penance to take away superfluity of
things delicate or soft, but it is penance when, in the
measure of sleep that we allow ourselves, something is
taken away from what is fitting. . . . The third way is
to chastise the flesh, to wit, by putting it to sensible
pain, which is inflicted by wearing hair shirts, or
cords, or iron chains on the bare flesh, by scourging
oneself, or wounding oneself, and by other modes of
austerities. What seems the more suitable and safe
thing in penance is for the pain to be sensible in the
flesh, without penetrating to the bones, so that it may
cause pain and not injury. Wherefore it seems more
fitting to scourge oneself with thin cords, which cause

pain externally, rather than in any other way, which may cause serious injury internally.'

The exercise begins with a preparatory prayer and two preludes. The first prelude consists in what is called the composition of place. The exercitant forms for himself a picture of the scene which is to be the subject of his meditation, the temple or mountain, for example, where Jesus Christ is found. In meditation of the invisible, as of sins, 'the composition will be to see with the eye of the imagination and consider my soul imprisoned in this corruptible body, and my whole compound self in this vale of tears as in banishment among brute animals.' In the second prelude the exercitant is to ask for what he wishes from the meditation. If his meditation is on the Resurrection he is to ask for joy with Christ rejoicing; if it is on the Passion he is to ask for pains, tears and torment with Christ tormented. The exercise ends with a colloquy in which the exercitant has to consider himself in the presence of Christ crucified and this is made 'as one friend speaks to another, or a servant to his master, now asking some favour, now reproaching oneself for some evil done, now speaking of one's own affairs and asking advice upon them.'

A Pater Noster brings the exercise to a fit conclusion. The first week contains five exercises. The first of these deals with the sin of the angels, the sin of Adam and Eve and the mortal sins of individuals. The second is a consideration of one's own sins. These are repeated during the third and fourth exercises. The fifth is concerned with hell.

I have an edition of the Spiritual Exercises in Spanish in which the Editor, Father Ramon Garcia, S.J., has charitably sought to make the way of the exercitant easier by describing for him in considerable detail the composition of place and by giving him the matter of his meditation in such a manner as to make it an intellectual exercise of no great severity. When he comes to the meditation of hell he displays a realistic fancy that is truly Spanish. Hell, he says, is like a very dark prison or a cavern of fire and intolerable smoke. With the eyes of his fancy the penitent must see the terrible flames and the souls enclosed as it were in bodies of fire. 'Look,' he cries, 'look at the unhappy creatures writhing in the burning flames, their hair standing on end, their eyes starting out of their heads, their aspect horrible, biting their hands, and with sweats and anguish of death and a thousand times worse than death. Look at the devils of frightful mien, not now tempting the wretched with thoughts of pleasure, but tormenting them like ruthless torturers. See how they mock and deride them, hit, strike and tear them with insatiable rage; for they are their slaves and they are in their power for sufferance as in the world they were in their power for sin. Apply your ears and listen to the tumult and perpetual confusion of those infernal dungeons. If when a house is burnt down the cries and the turmoil are so great, what will be the clamour of these innumerable people who burn in living fire?' Now by an effort of imagination making use of his sense of smell the penitent becomes conscious of the sulphurous smoke and stench of the sink of hell. The pestilential air stinks in his nostrils. It is the rank atmosphere of a prison that has no vent; it is worse than the exhalation of a dungeon; it is far more disgusting than the depth of an open grave. The bodies of the damned are alive with worms and emit more putrescence than corpses, so that one would be enough to poison a whole countryside. 'What then will be the stink of this horrible prison crammed with so many abominable bodies? We must reflect that the depth of hell is like a lake of liquid sulphur from which rise heavy vapours, and they, since they have no issue, condense; and this noxious venom, so heavy that it is almost palpable, the wretches with mortal agony continually breathe. That unhappy place is an abyss into which, after the Day of Judgment, will fall the putridity, the poison and the ordure of the whole extension of the earth so that it will be like an unfathomable latrine in which the condemned will find themselves submerged. Think what will be the stench of so much filth there commingled and agglomerated. Think also of the bitter, stinging tears that perpetually flow from the eyes of the damned, furrowing and burning their faces. If in our own bodies, as the result of a sudden shock, or from a paroxysm of anger, we may have indigestion, effusion of bile, bad blood, bitter taste, stinking breath, cough, nausea, vomiting and other miseries of great affliction to such as suffer them, and of no little distress and disgust to such as see them, what will be the mouth and breath of the damned? There is nothing in the world so repulsive, nor stink with which it can be compared. To this must be added the worm of conscience that is ever gnawing their entrails and spewing into them bitter gall and constant remorse.'

'And what,' asks Father Ramon, 'shall we say of the thirst and hunger that torment them?' Much. Raging is the thirst caused by the heat and the ceaseless wailing. For centuries the rich miser has had his gullet parched and his tongue hanging out of his mouth with the hankering for a drop of water, and never shall he get it, for in that place there is nothing to drink but gall of dragons, poison of asps, boiling pitch and liquid sulphur. They are hungry with a brutal hunger, the damned, and without respite suffer from languor, inanition and a very active craving to eat something, but there is nothing for them to eat but wormwood, pitch, and molten lead that burns their entrails.

'Now touch with the touch of imagination the fire that crucifies the souls of the damned. Acute and very fearful is the pain it causes. The fire of this world is like the fire in a picture compared with that; for it is the wrath of God that lights it and maintains it, so that it shall be a terrible instrument of his just vengeance.

The damned live plunged in this, like fish in water, or rather (better, says my author) penetrated as by a red-hot coal, the flames entering their throats, veins, muscles, bones, entrails and all their vitals. It combines and symbolises all the aches and pains that can afflict and torment our flesh and our spirit: wounds, convulsions, agonies, the ills of gout and stone, blows, whippings, chains, gallows, nippers, swords, wheels and hooks. It likewise torments the soul. One cannot understand how; but this is certain that, with a formidable activity, it penetrates and atrociously tortures the very spirit; since our faith teaches that the demons also burn and suffer from the pain of fire.'

Having given the reader this lively and impressive picture of the fate in store for the sinner the author points out that it is everlasting. The damned are eternal not only in their souls but also in their bodies. They will long for death, but death will flee from them; indeed, the rage to destroy themselves will cause them fearful agony since they perceive that they cannot die. Their torments are not only everlasting, but they continue for ever without interruption; they are invariable, without diminution; they do not cease for an hour, for a moment; nor is there any alleviation. And though so long and so unceasing, custom does not mitigate them and so render the suffering less intolerable. Every day they are as new and return with new exacerbation.

Then in a passage that seems to me of considerable

power the good Father pauses to consider the meaning of eternity. Eternity lasts for ever. Eternity is unending. 'In order to form a conception of so terrible a thing, let us embrace in our imagination any number of years, or millions of years, and we shall find that after they have passed eternity remains entire. As many millions of years may pass over the damned as drops of water have fallen upon the earth, and shall fall to the end of the world, and as many drops of water as there are in all the seas on the planet. As many millions of years as there have been leaves, are or shall be, on all the trees and plants in the world. As many millions of years as there are rays of the sun, atoms in the air and sands of the sea. And after there has passed this incalculable number of years, the torments of these unhappy creatures shall continue, as though they were but beginning, as though it were the first day; and eternity and suffering will remain whole as though not one second had passed.

'What do you say to this, my soul? If in your soft bed it is so painful to you to pass a long night of sleeplessness and pain, waiting eagerly for the relief of dawn, what will you feel in that eternal night upon which the dawn never breaks, during which you will never have an instant of refreshment, during which you will never see a ray of hope?'

This meditation ends the first week. The exercitant makes a general confession and receives absolution.

Before going further I should like to narrate a little

story that is told by Don José Muñoz San Roman and that the reader can take as he likes. The people of a certain village in Andalusia were tired of the Lenten preacher who sought every year to bring them to repentance with sermons that they knew by heart; so the mayor, to give them a treat, secured for the usual discourses the services of a friar whose fame had reached even that secluded spot. His arrival was awaited with eagerness and all the inhabitants came out into the streets to welcome him. The authorities, lay and ecclesiastical, met him at the railway; and the women of the place, surrounding the mayor's lady, stationed themselves at the foot of the Cross that stood at the entrance to the village. The preacher made his entry amid the acclamations of the multitude. They crowded into the church. So that they should not miss a single one of his winged words they struggled to get as near the pulpit as possible, and when he ascended it a tremor of curiosity and expectation passed through the congregation. His manner was humble as he entered into his exordium and his words were mild; but then raising his voice and changing his tone he gave on a sudden a great cry. Remorse seized and shattered him, anger beetled his brows, terror made him quail and then again he was suffocated with rage. His gestures were abundant and dramatic. And such was the language with which he described the affronts that were suffered during the Passion by Jesus Christ and the anguish that on their account afflicted the Blessed Virgin that the people were dissolved into bitter and noisy tears. Such was the orator's eloquence and in so vivid colours did he depict the Passion of the Redeemer that many of the faithful fainted and some had convulsions. The mayor's wife fell to the floor in a fit to the consternation of those around her and to the mayor's very natural concern. The whole congregation was the prey to an ungovernable agitation.

The preacher at last perceived what was happening. He was very much surprised. The congregation, outraged at the condition to which he had reduced them, were about to rush the pulpit and the unfortunate man hardly knew how to stem the torrent of indignation he had aroused. He besought his listeners to calm themselves, for there was an uproar, and begged for silence. When at last he was able to make himself heard, he said:

'But, my brethren, reflect that all this that I tell you happened many years ago. And it may be that it never happened at all.'

With these consoling words he was able to calm the perturbed spirits of his congregation.

One of the most interesting things to my mind in the Spiritual Exercises is the method of combating sin called Particular and General Examen. The particular examen deals with special sins; the exercitant performs it three times a day; on rising, when he resolves to be on his guard against the sin of which he wishes to amend himself; after dinner, when he marks with dots on a line the number of times he has committed it; and after supper, when he makes dots on a lower line for each subsequent trespass. This he repeats every day, comparing the numbers of dots from day to day. A curious detail is the advice to put his hand to his breast each time he offends, 'which may be done even in company without anyone noticing what he is doing.' The General Examen, as its name suggests, is a general examination of conscience.

The first week is concerned with sin, the second with contemplation on the life of the Eternal King, the third with contemplation on the Passion of Christ and the fourth on the Resurrection. The second week is the culminating point of the exercises, for it leads to the election of a state of life. The third and fourth week confirm and fortify the exercitant in the resolutions he has then made.

When you look at the exercises as a whole you cannot but observe how marvellously they are devised to effect their object. Saint Ignatius is an artist who forms living souls after his own image. He creates them as the poet creates a poem. But he seeks to strengthen the character rather than to develop the intelligence. Blind obedience was what he claimed and he allowed to none the pleasant freedom of thinking for himself. We know now how great is the value of suggestion and what strange things may be achieved by its power. Saint Ignatius learnt its secrets in his own person. The physical condition to which the exercitant is reduced and the circumstances in which he performs the exercises produce in him a state of passivity in which he is very ready to receive the desired impressions. One can well imagine that after this shattering experience the spirit must for ever lose its resilience. It is said that the result of the first week is to reduce the neophyte to utter prostration. Contrition saddens, shame and fear harrow him. Not only is he terrified by the frightful pictures on which his mind has dwelt, he has been weakened by lack of food and exhausted by want of sleep. He has been brought to such despair that he does not know where to fly for relief. Then a new ideal is set before him, the ideal of Christ; and to this, his will broken, he is led to sacrifice himself with a joyful heart. It has been said that no heretic who performed the exercises in the indicated way could fail, not only to become a Catholic, but to seek refuge in the Company of Jesus. It is said that the Jesuits who were sent on their dangerous missions to protestant England, before starting were set a special exercise in which (the composition of place) they were bidden with their mind's eye to picture to themselves the prison into which they might be cast, the grim chamber where horrible torture would be inflicted upon them, and the place of execution where amid frightful torments they would achieve the crown of martyrdom.

They were enjoined in imagination to feel the bitter cold of the dungeon and its noisome stench, the heavy chains that galled their flesh, the red-hot irons that seared it, the rack that tore their joints and the blows that mangled their limbs; and then, in agony, the sharpness of the knife that disembowelled them, the acrid smoke that choked their lungs and the flames that intolerably burned their living flesh. And such was the anguish of this exercise that when they had at last to submit to the reality they did so, not only without fear, but in complete insensibility. They had already endured all that the mortal body and the immortal soul could endure. And if it is not true and they suffered like other men, they did not survive to say so.

I had the curiosity on one occasion to attempt to do one of the exercises myself. It was a singular experience. I began with the composition of place. It seems simple enough, but I found it none too easy, and I am not surprised that the commentators have seen the necessity of providing the exercitant with particulars circumstantial enough to eke out a halting fancy. But I found this child's play compared with the meditation. It is true that I had not prepared myself by fasting or corporal penance, and grace was certainly not vouchsafed me. To me it was incredibly difficult to fix my mind on a subject and concentrate on it without distraction. I was for ever wandering along by-paths and down crooked ways. I could think of anything but what I wanted to. I suppose mathematicians and philosophers can control the flow of their ideas and have no difficulty in directing their reflections towards the end they have in view. With most of us the mind is discursive and the labour of pursuing a train of thought, step by step, without deviation, is very severe. I think a good deal, and, I am inclined to believe, with lucidity, but I cannot think to order: notions and impressions come at haphazard, they are stored away in the subconscious and emerge when they are needed, sifted, combined and elaborated, by no effort that I am aware of: to endeavour then deliberately to picture to myself a series of events and to feel the emotions that moved the actors in them when they experienced them was an exercise of will that I found myself almost incapable of. My spirit (animula vagula) seemed to be compassed about by obstacles that were almost material and it fluttered here and there in a desperate anxiety to escape. The violence to which I subjected my imagination paralysed it. I felt like a bird struggling in a net. My head seemed to be constricted in an iron band and I had such a peculiar feeling in the pit of my stomach I thought I was going to be sick.

Saint Ignatius instructed the exercitant to repeat the same meditation twice and sometimes three times; but whether he did this because he knew from his own experience how difficult the performance was or whether he wished only to confirm its effect I do not know. It must then be an exercise of extreme severity. For though we can turn our thoughts again to a subject that has occupied us and it may be think of it more profoundly, we cannot by an effort of will feel again an emotion that we have felt before; otherwise, I suppose, none of us would cause others the pain of ceasing to love them. The attempt must tear the nerves to pieces. But I cannot persuade myself that meditation forced upon the mind is likely to give rise to fresh and inspiring notions. I should have thought rather that by such a practice the spirit was enslaved and cowed, while the happy flow of fancy was for ever stemmed. It may be that this is what Saint Ignatius aimed at. If so the Spiritual Exercises are the most wonderful method that has ever been devised to gain control over that vagabond, unstable and wilful thing, the soul of man.

Considering that their effect has been achieved through a constant and ruthless appeal to terror and shame it is surprising to observe that the last contemplation of all is a contemplation of love.

IV

MANY years ago I wrote a book about Andalusia, but I am bitterly conscious of its defects. It is called The Land of the Blessed Virgin. In those days, at the end of the nineteenth century, the young were more immature than at present; they had not the knowing, clever way of concealing their ignorance that now fills with admiration those who have occasion to read their works. I was but twenty-three when I went to Seville. I had spent five years in a London hospital and for the first time in my life was my own master. I have been back to Spain a dozen times since then; it has never ceased to possess for me the glamour of those first few months of heavenly freedom. I had no ties and no responsibilities. I had no care in the world but to write well; I did not know then what severe labour and what harassing bondage this entailed. I wandered about the country, enthusiastic with all the new sights I saw, but my enthusiasm (though I did not know it) was perfectly conventional. It is curious how seldom youth looks at the world with the fresh and direct gaze that you would have expected to come naturally to it; whether from diffidence or timidity it looks upon what it has never seen before with alien eyes. Perhaps a certain sophistication is needed before one can see things for oneself. Such certainly was the case with me. My feelings were genuine enough, but they were the feelings of the travellers who had gone before me. I saw what Borrow and Richard Ford, Théophile Gautier and Mérimée had seen.

Presently I went for a trip on horseback. At that time the only means of communication between one region and another was the railway, for the roads were impassable to wheeled traffic, and if you wanted to see places that were not on the line you had to ride. When I came back I thought it would be a good exercise to write an account of the excursion. In fiction the manner of your writing is conditioned by your matter. You cannot write in the same way if you are describing an incident as if you are analysing a state of mind; dialogue, which you aim at making as natural as possible, breaks the pattern; it is only in the essay or in the book of travel that you can attempt a sustained effect. It is very good for the novelist now and again to try his hand at something of the sort.

But when I had done this as best I could I did not know what to do with it. I was never the sort of writer who is content to shut up his work in a drawer. I fell very pleasantly in love while I was in Seville and the possibility had been running in my mind of turning this experience to account by writing a novel in which I might give a romanticised, but ironic, account of it. For even then, not slow to see my own absurdity, I was conscious that I had been made a very pretty fool of. It offered me an opportunity of describing the cathedral, certain pictures, a bull-fight and the easy, attractive life of Seville. But I hesitated, thinking people would say it was merely an imitation of Pierre Loti (which indeed it would have been) who was then very much read and who had done that sort of thing very delightfully and in exquisite French This was foolish of me. I did not know that in the next thirty years no less than three English writers (and several American) were going to achieve eminence by imitating Anatole France I might safely have written this book, and had it proved a success I could have followed it up with agreeably humorous and sentimental accounts of an affair of the heart in every country in Europe. I might now enjoy a great reputation as a writer of charm, sensibility and discrimination. I refrained. But sooner than waste the narrative I had written of my ride I wrote a description of Seville and what I had seen there, added to it, to give it a sort of completeness, sketches of other places in Andalusia and in this way got together enough material to make a little book.

It was crude and gushing. Thinking it over as the years went by I was persuaded that I could do better and each time I went to Spain I was tempted to try again. But I did not want to write another book of travel. Too many travellers already have travelled in Spain. All the writer can do is to describe his own sensations and there is little likelihood that his descriptions will call up sensations that represent with any exactness the objects he has tried to depict.

The streets of Santiago de Compostela are narrow, paved with great blocks worn smooth by the tread of generations; and they go up and down and wind this way and that. But in the end they all lead to the Cathedral which was the goal for so many centuries of innumerable pilgrims. Now, the façade of this is one of the great sights of the world. It is of grey stone, but here and there yellow with lichen, and in some places are patches of green where a hardy little shrub has managed to attach itself. It is wonderfully impressive against dark and threatening clouds (it rains a great deal in Santiago) but when the sun shines and the sky is blue it has the colour of honey. The architecture is luxuriant, but its heroic grandeur prevents it from being tiresome and the perfect balance of the decorative motives gives an impression of an almost classic severity. It is like a purple patch in Chapman's Homer. I cannot but think that the architect must have felt a pang at his heart when he looked at the finished façade and knew that it was magnificent. It is not one of those sights that insinuate their charm and captivate you only after long acquaintance: it takes you by storm. It remains in the mind as a permanent possession and the spirit is enriched by the recollection of it. But words cannot reproduce the splendour of those towers and the satisfactoriness of that opulent symmetry. A glance at a photograph is more likely to give you its peculiar thrill than half a dozen pages of careful description. No, I did not want to write a book of travel.

Several subjects floated about in my mind and I amused myself by considering what I could make of them. For some time I was attracted by Ponce de Leon, the discoverer of Florida; for the conquistadores set out on their perilous journeys to the new-discovered lands on the other side of the Atlantic to acquire wealth, but he, more romantically, to find the spring of eternal youth. I invented a story that I liked. Its disadvantage was that it led me overseas, and I wanted to stay in Spain. Then my fancy was taken with the little court that the Dukes of Alba held at Alba de Tormes. They lived magnificently, cultivating the arts; and here, under their protection, the valorous and charming poet Garcilaso de la Vega spent some part of his short and glorious life. I went to Alba. The town runs up the hill by the side of the river. The streets are deserted and chickens run about them; they are paved with rough cobbles so that walking is painful. The houses are small and plain, whitewashed or mud-coloured, and on one or two of the better ones is a coat of arms over the door. But it gives you an odd thrill to catch sight of the name of the street you are walking through; it is called Calle de los Pages. Nothing remains of the great villa decorated by painters and sculptors from Italy and furnished with the spoils of conquered countries, but a sombre tower that stands on the top of a hill. I suppose the gardens, famous in their day, the scene of poetic contests, where the Italianate writers conversed of their art and musicians played the viol and the lute, stretched down to the quiet, winding river; but I could find no trace of them and such of the inhabitants as I asked knew nothing of them. My imagination rebelled against the labour of reconstructing that past life and those dead glories from materials so scanty.

Besides, I wanted a subject that gave me elbow room. I did not want to be confined to the palace of a great nobleman and the doings of cultured persons. I wanted a theme that gave me the opportunity to show the rich and varied life that you read of in the picaresque novels. I wanted to deal with the theatre, for the drama in Spain's golden age, the short period that began with Lazarillo de Tormes and ended with Calderon, was not only the national passion but the most characteristic expression of the nation's artistic endeavours. For a little while I played with the notion of writing a novel about Agustin de Rojas, an actor who has left in El Viage Entretenido, not only a graphic account of the stage in his day and the life of a strolling player, but in his devil-may-care account of his own affairs a very sufficient portrait of himself. Even in the Spain of that period it would be difficult to find a man who led a more picturesque life. The son of Diego de Villadiego, a gentleman of birth, and of Luisa de Rojas, whose name, following a Spanish custom not uncommon at the time, he generally used, Agustin was born in Madrid about 1577. At nine years old he was a page in an illustrious house and at fourteen, desiring to see the world and enjoy adventure, he ran away to Seville to become a soldier. He was in garrison for a while at Castilleja de la Cuesta and then set sail for France. He landed in Brittany. For two years he was engaged in various warlike operations, gaining for himself much glory and some profit, and then, sailing for Nantes on a French ship, was taken prisoner. He was brought to La Rochelle and there put to serve a certain Monsieur de Fontena till he was exchanged with his companions in slavery for natives of La Rochelle who were rowing in the Spanish galleys. He spent two years more privateering against English ships and at last landed in Santander. He made his way to Madrid where he contracted an illness from which he nearly died.

On his recovery he seems to have gone to sea again in the royal galleys and eventually took his discharge at Malaga. He entered the service of a paymaster and went with him to Granada. He was then twenty-two. He had already seen the chief cities of Italy. In Granada things went well with him and he provided himself with fine clothes and chains of solid gold. But losing his place he returned to Malaga and here had the strangest of his adventures. Having killed a man in a brawl he sought sanctuary in the church of St. John. The police surrounded it and he stayed there for two days. He was starving with hunger. Then, since the watch was somewhat relaxed, risking everything and determined on any extremity, he made a bolt for it. But by good fortune he stumbled upon a very beautiful woman who, carried off her feet by his handsome face and gallant bearing, when she heard of his intention persuaded him to return to the safety of the church. It cost her three hundred ducats to get him out of his scrape, but the payment of such a sum left her destitute. Rojas took her to his lodgings and to get her food begged for alms at night, wrote sermons for a friar of the Monastery of St. Augustine (for each of which he was paid with a dish of meat and a pound of bread) stole capes and robbed orchards and vineyards. How the affair ended is uncertain, for at this point of his story the narrator's emotion very unfortunately prevented him from continuing.

But it seems to have been then that he decided to go on the stage. He wandered with one company and another through Spain, accompanied possibly by the beautiful woman who had saved him from the gallows. It happened not infrequently that the theatres were closed, either on account of the pestilence or the death of a royal personage, and on one such occasion, being then in Granada, he opened a haber-dashery which was highly successful. He led this life for three years and then a catastrophe befell him. His mistress left him. 'At length,' he wrote later to some friends in Seville, 'I was abandoned by the most lovely angel in the world and the unkindest shepherdess that heaven ever created. Wretched at her cruelty I confess that I was beset by such sore pain that I was on the point of killing myself.' He calls the traitress Elisa, but whether it is the heroine of the adventure at Malaga or another there is no knowing. One hopes it was, for it makes a better story. Heart-broken, Rojas repaired to the mountains of Cordova, where he joined himself to the hermits who inhabited their caves, and with penance and prayer sought to wean himself from the vanity of the world. But he was not of a temper to spend his life in such morti-fication and after a time he returned to the world that had, all in all, not treated him too badly. He married presently, and since as an actor he could not have saved money and he had some, he must very prudently have chosen a wife with means. But an unfortunate lawsuit deprived him of a considerable part of his fortune, whereupon he entered the service of a Genoese, merchant or banker, who robbed him of the rest. He was for a short time in prison, was attacked and nearly killed by ruffians in Seville, and is last heard of as a scrivener and notary to the Bishop of Zamora.

He was then thirty-three.

An adventurous and romantic life. It provided me with pretty well everything I needed; Rojas had charm, humour and a pretty gift for writing light verse. He was brave. He was of notable beauty. He loved fine clothes and splendid ornaments; and on account of this foible was known to his friends as the Cavalier of the Miracles, since without a penny to bless himself with he never wanted for rich apparel. He had the deep, religious sense that was characteristic of the Spaniard of the day, and when misfortunes fell upon him he welcomed them as a bounty granted by the hand of God for the good and glory of his soul.

But I was a little afraid of Agustin de Rojas. He was somewhat too much a man of action for my purpose. When a writer falls into the hands of so vivid a personality as this, he can never be sure that he will not be led along paths he has no wish to tread. A fellow of this sort can very well take things into his own control and give occasion to a book quite different from that which the author had proposed to write. Nor, with my long experience, did I fail to notice that in the love affair which seems to have been the culminating point of Agustin's life, it was the woman who was the more interesting party. If it was one and the same woman who ruined herself to save his life, lived with him in miserable poverty, and then left him and nearly broke his heart, a singular story emerges. Only a very dull novelist could fail to be taken by this woman of swift passion and reckless temper. Generous and impulsive, she was willing for love's sake to abandon the security which they say women seek above all else and she was indifferent to the extreme of poverty. She was gallant, determined and adventurous. She found the love that had seemed worth every sacrifice die in her heart; and ruthlessly, with the decision that must have characterised her, she left her lover for another. Tender and cruel, faithful and fickle, self-possessed and unrestrained, she must have been an amazing creature.

That was not the subject I wanted. I wanted a freer hand. I thought I should be much better off with a character of my own invention. I did not see why I should not make my hero a young Catholic Scot, who had come to seek his fortune under the King of Spain, or the kinsman to an ambassador accredited to the Court of Madrid by the aged Queen Elizabeth. Such a one I could conduct with verisimilitude through the different worlds that interested me. I wished to concern myself not a little with my hero's spiritual adventures, and it seemed to me that if I made him a reflective, observant youth, well furnished with the culture of the day, I should have a very good opportunity to study the various aspects of the Spanish mind at the moment I proposed to deal with. This was the beginning of the reign of Philip III.

Lope de Vega was the idol of the Spanish stage. He ruled his pasteboard kingdom despotically and brooked no rivals. Cervantes had not published Don Quixote, but much of the first part was written and he had read some chapters to his friends. El Greco, living in Toledo with no little splendour, had freed himself at last from his long bondage to the Venetians, and in his old age returning to the inspiration of his Cretan youth, was painting the most extraordinary of his pictures. Mateo Aleman had written Guzman de Alfarache, the most popular of the picaresque novels, and Vicente Espinel was turning over in his cynical old head the charming Life of Marcos de Obregon. You might still meet learned men and great ladies who had talked with the Blessed Teresa de Jesus and there were students in Salamanca who had listened to the lectures of Fray Luis de Leon. The Spaniards were the proudest people in the world. Though ruined and starving they thought themselves still as powerful as when Charles V took the King of France prisoner at Pavia, and though bled white to crush the heretic and keep the faith unsullied they looked upon the sacrifices their foolish kings demanded of them as no more than their due. Noblesse oblige.

I did not dislike my idea. I thought I could make something of it and so set to work. I had read a good deal of Spanish literature in the many years that had passed since first I crossed the Pyrenees, but I had read only for my amusement. Now I started on it again after a more systematic fashion.

V

IT would be absurd in a little book of this sort, written for my own instruction and amusement, to give a list of the authorities I have consulted; but all the same I should not be easy in my mind unless I acknowledged my debt to the scholarly works of the Professors Altamira and Alison Peers and the advantage I have taken of the industry of Mr. Aubrey Bell, Herr Ludwig Pfandl and Dr. Rennert. These erudite persons have taught me a great deal and in return I am going to give them a little information that will be new to them. At all events there is no trace in any of their learned books that the matter has ever attracted their attention. I am going to tell them something about food in Spain.

Avila is a city in which it should be pleasant to linger. There is nothing much to do there and little to see. The walls, greatly restored, are like the walls of an old city in a book of hours. The neat, round towers placed at regular intervals look like the trim curls of a seventeenth century peruke. The cathedral with its fortress-like air has not much to offer you but an effect of sombreness, and its Gothic porches and windows are not so good as many that you have seen elsewhere. Besides, now we are all a little bored with Gothic architecture. But the houses of the old hidalgos have still kept something of their grave stateliness; those grand escutcheons over the doorways are very impressive. A silent city. There are many streets in which you may stand for an hour without seeing a passer-by. The men in Avila wear black and the women are in deep mourning. The air even in summer has a certain sharpness; in spring and autumn the wind blows bitter, and in winter the cold is severe. It is Castile with its reserve, its taciturnity and its ceremonial stiffness. But the hotel is one of the worst in Spain. The rooms are bare and comfortless, it is none too clean and it smells; the food, served in a grim, large dining-room in which there is a harsh blaze of electric light, is frightful; one uneatable dish follows another, thrown at you by a slovenly waiter with dirty hands, on cold plates, and the cellar can provide hardly any of the wines the list offers.

I can eat almost anything, if not with pleasure, without distaste, and a bad dinner does nothing to disturb my serenity. I can say with truth that I have a soul above food, but alas, though my spirit is strong my flesh is weak, and a poor meal, which I have devoured without complaint, will make me as sick as a dog for a week. That body which Fray Roldan spoke of as the asinillo, the little donkey, will let my dancing spirit take no liberties with it. On one such occasion in Avila, having at last fallen asleep after tossing from side to side on my hard bed for hours, I was awakened by the crowing of a cock, and a few minutes later I heard the sudden hubbub of a bell. It was quite startling in that deep night. It occurred to me that they must be ringing for early mass. I got up, slipped a pair of trousers over my pyjamas and put on a great coat; the night-porter opened the door for me and I walked across the street. The cathedral was in darkness but for one chapel in which burned an electric light. A sacristan, muffled up in a cloak, with a grey woollen scarf over his mouth and nose, was lighting the candles. I saw the backs of three women in black kneeling before the altar. A peasant-woman, with a basket on her arm and a hand-kerchief over her head, came along just before the priest. He seemed to be in a hurry, a fat little man with grey hair and an earthy face; he walked so quickly that the acolyte behind him was almost running. As he uttered the first words of the mass, gabbling un-intelligibly in a low voice, a man stepped out of the darkness. I glanced at him with surprise. I had not thought that anyone was there but those four women. He was a tall, thin man, with a voluminous cloak draped round him; he had flashing eyes under bushy eyebrows, a big hooked nose and an immense head of long, curling, grey hair; his face was harsh and rugged. So might have looked one of the old conquistadores. He did not kneel. He stood motionless, his mouth tight-closed, with his strange eyes fixed on the altar. I wondered what he did there. It was bitterly cold. I felt very sick. I went back to the hotel and they gave me goat's milk with my coffee and rancid butter with my bread. It was too much.

You must not be blamed then if in Avila you say that it is impossible to get a decent meal in Spain. But it is an error. You can eat very well in Spain, only you must know where to go and how to set about it. In the first place you must decide to make your meal of a single dish and it may be that this is a very wise thing. For thus you do not overeat. However good one dish is you can only eat as much as will satisfy your hunger.

The Spaniards are coarse, but sparing eaters. They do not seem to mind if their food is bad and ill-cooked, they will eat fish that is far from fresh, and bollito and garbanzos, boiled beef and chick peas, monotonous fare, day after day without disgust. They have always been frugal. Indeed one of the great virtues of the Spanish soldier was that he could march and fight on so little food that you would have thought it hardly enough to keep body and soul together. The traveller, you read in the picaresque novels, was content to make a meal on a hunk of bread and an onion. On the other hand it must be admitted that when it came to a feast their capacity was enormous. When Sempronio and Parmeno wanted to offer their two girl friends and the old bawd Celestina a supper they sent along (for five persons) a ham, six pairs of young chickens and some pigeons, Murviedo wine and white bread. When I first went to Spain it was difficult, except in one or two hotels in Madrid, Barcelona and Seville where they made a poor imitation of French rolls, to get any bread except a sort of double roll of a doughy white substance unappetising to look at, tasteless to eat and heavy on the stomach. Now you can get French bread in any town of consequence, but it is neither crisp nor savoury. If you want good bread you must go to some of the mountain villages in the north, where, if you are lucky enough to get in just when it comes from the baker's, you may eat a loaf of rye bread, beautiful in colour and sweet-smelling, with a crust that crumbles in the mouth deliciously. With this and some butter—almost unobtainable in Spain thirty years ago, but now to be found everywhere—a few olives, anchovies and a goat cheese you can make a repast fit for a king.

Of course no one who has any sense will eat the table d'hôte meals provided in hotels. They are long and bad after the French style in the first-class hotels; they are long and no worse after the Spanish style in the second-class. Their monotony is deplorable. In both you will get the same insipid clear soup; and you will seldom see any fish but the coarse, tough, savourless merluza. Hake! There is only one good soup in Spain, a soup of rice and vegetables and little bits of meat. It is called tres quartos de ora. You must order it beforehand, for as its name implies it takes three quarters of an hour to make; and of course not at an hotel, but in some little restaurant in a side street. It is a meal in itself, and a very good one.

But even in the hotels, in those not quite of the first class that is, if they are not very busy and you will talk it over in a friendly way with the head waiter or the cook, you can often get very good things to eat. Thus at Alicante, one of those agreeable towns in which there is nothing whatever to see, to which I went in the dead season, I got an arroz à la Valenciana which was perfect. I drank the local wine with it, a pale wine, very delicious, with a faint flavour of muscatel. I forgot to say that you will never like Spanish fare unless you can stomach food cooked in oil; if you insist that everything you eat should be cooked in butter then you must expect nothing from Spain but the gratifications of the spirit; the table can have no pleasures to offer you.

Arroz à la Valenciana is the local dish of Valencia and I dare say it was invented in that dull and noisy city. When Ruy Dias de Bivar conquered Valencia he proceeded according to the poem as follows:

'*With my Cid to the Alcazar went straight his wife and daughters.*
Once there he led them to the highest point of all,
Where did fair eyes look on all sides around.
At their feet they behold the city, Valencia where it lies,
And yonder on the other side within their view is the sea.'

I like to think that then he took them by the hand and led them to where was waiting for them a goodly dish of arroz à la Valenciana. I wish that Professor Peers who spent some months there, I believe, had for a little while diverted his erudite studies on El Cid Campeador (an engaging ruffian) to look into the origins of this tasty dish. I should like to know whether it was the discovery of a Moor of genius, or whether it invented itself by accident, simultaneously, in the kitchens of a hundred Moorish housewives. Though it is called after Valencia it is eaten all along the coast from Barcelona to Malaga. In Andalusia it is called paella. It is never bad and sometimes it is of an excellence that surpasses belief. Rice is of course its foundation, saffron and red peppers give it a Spanish tang; it has chicken in it, clams, mussels, prawns and I know not what. It takes a long time to make and is a great deal of trouble. It is worth the time and worth the trouble. But the best arroz I ever ate was at Tarragona.

Tarragona has a cathedral that is grey and austere, very plain, with immense, severe pillars; it is like a fortress; a place of worship for headstrong, violent and cruel men. The night falls early within its walls and then the columns in the aisles seem to squat down on themselves and darkness shrouds the Gothic arches. It terrifies you. It is like a dungeon. I was there last on a Monday in Holy Week and from the pulpit a preacher was delivering a Lenten sermon. Two or three naked

electric globes threw a cold light that cut the outline of
the columns against the darkness as though with
scissors. It only just fell upon the crowd, mostly
women, who sat, between the chancel and the choir,
huddled together as though they cowered in fear of a
foe that besieged the city. With violent gestures, in a
loud, scolding voice, the preacher poured forth with
extreme rapidity a torrent of denunciation. Each angry,
florid phrase was like a blow and one blow followed
another with vicious insistence. From the farthest end
of the majestic church, winding about the columns and
curling round the groining of the arches, down the great
austere nave and along the dungeon-like aisles, that
rasping, shrewish voice pursued you.

But a devout admirer had entertained the preacher at
luncheon that day in the hotel in which I was staying.
It was quite a party. There were the host's grey-haired
and corpulent wife, his two sons with their wives, or his
two daughters with their husbands (I could only guess),
and eight or nine children of various ages, whom I tried
to sort out. The preacher tucked in to the arroz like one
o'clock. It comforted me at that moment to remember
this. It was a bad, bad world, but a merciful pro-
vidence had allowed occasional alleviations to the
miserable lot of man, and among these must un-
doubtedly be placed arroz à la Valenciana as we had both
eaten it that noon at Tarragona.

In almost every town in Spain you can find a res-

taurant in which you can eat well enough to satisfy an
exigent taste. In Madrid you can find half a dozen.
But there is one that should be known to all travellers.
It is in the Plaza Herradores. It is bare and comfortless;
you sit on a hard chair; the linen is coarse and the light
is harsh. But you do not care, for your mouth waters
with pleasant anticipation: you are going to eat sucking-
pig. Four or five of them lie on a dish in the window,
with cut throats, and they look so like newborn babies
that it gives you quite a turn. But you must avert your
mind resolutely from this notion. They are killed at
three weeks old. It is impossible to describe how
exquisite they are, how tender, how succulent, how
juicy, and what spiritual ecstasy there is in the crackling:
just as there is nothing really to say about a symphony,
you must listen to it; so there is nothing to be said about
a sucking-pig, you must eat it.

For a reason that I have never been able to discover
you eat much better in the north of a country than in the
south. The English cherish the ingenuous notion that
you can eat well anywhere in France. It is not true.
They think that you can go to no restaurant in France, to
no hotel, in which you cannot get a good omelette. It is
not true. You cannot eat well south of Vienne. And in
Andalusia you eat romantically rather than to the
satisfaction of your palate. My thoughts wander back
to a tavern in Seville, just off the Sierpes, where the
manzanilla was good and the innkeeper got his hams

from Estramadura. You used to go there late at night, after the zarzuela at the theatre was over, and order yourself half a portion of smoked ham and a dish of black, juicy olives. A boy would cut across the street and bring you from the cook-shop a plate of fried fish. You sat in a little cubicle, on a wooden bench, with a companion (for who can eat alone?) and in the next cubicle, if you were in luck, there would be a little party, one of the men with a guitar, and after a long introductory twanging a woman broke into the melancholy, Moorish wail of a seguidilla. Ole, Ole!

The Spanish are very fond of sea-food. The itinerant salesmen with their baskets of shrimps, huge prawns, clams and sea-urchins do a great trade as they wander from tavern to tavern. The fish in the fried fish shops is very fresh and provided of course that you do not mind its being cooked in oil, exceedingly good. But if you want to eat fish you must really go to Vigo. When, notwithstanding all I have written, I am inclined with melancholy to agree with those who say that you cannot eat well in Spain, I think of Vigo and tell myself that this is nonsense. Vigo is one of the few ports in Europe where you can get fish. Boulogne is another. There are none in England. I have never eaten a better luncheon in my life than I ate at Vigo. There was every variety of fish as hors d'œuvre, clams, prawns, mussels, anchovies and a dozen more, a shrimp omelette, and then a delicious fried fish that you knew had come out of the sea that very morning, kid, very tender and good, and two or three dishes to follow. But these, my hunger satisfied, I left untouched. It was a wonderful meal.

But Vigo, alas, does not hold for me only this charming memory; it holds for me also the memory of an opportunity missed, and I cannot think of it without some pricking of conscience. It was like this. I stopped at Vigo on my way from Santiago to Salamanca. 1 had discovered from the map that it was not easy to find one's way out of the town, and when after luncheon I was asking the porter of the hotel to direct me, a small boy came up and offered to show me. To my surprise, for Vigo is on the western coast of Spain, a little north of Portugal, he spoke in French and not only in French but in the unmistakable accent of the Midi. I asked him what this meant. He told me he was born in Marseilles. I bade him jump in the car and we drove off.

He said he was fourteen, but he was undersized and looked less. He was very thin, almost in rags, with a pinched, sallow face all eyes. In the intervals of directing us through narrow streets and round unexpected turnings he told me that he was a foundling who had been taken care of in the hospital in Marseilles for lost children. A few months before, because he was un-happy, he had run down to the harbour and stowed away in a sailing ship which he learnt was about to sail. He did not know whither she was bound. They did not

find him till they were well out at sea, and when they did
they beat him and put him to work in the cook's galley.
It was a French boat and he was afraid they would take
him back to France and return him to the hospital; so
when they touched at Vigo he ran away again and hid
himself till she sailed. He had nothing but the clothes he
stood up in, not a penny in his pocket, and no papers of
any sort to identify him. His only name was the name
they had given him at the hospital. I do not suppose
anyone could be more alone in the world.

'How do you live?' I asked him.

'Oh, I manage. I run errands. Sometimes someone
gives me a few coppers.'

'Don't you starve often?'

'Oh, I don't say I'm not hungry sometimes. I don't
care. I'd sooner die than go back to the hospital.'

'And where do you sleep?'

'In the street. It's all right in summer. It's cold in
winter, but I manage. I know a shed that's not locked
and I can get in there whenever I want to. You see, I
like my liberty.'

He had the meridional gift of the gab and he expressed himself with a fine flow of language, with
eloquent shrugs of his little thin shoulders and with
jaunty waves of the hand. He made light of everything.
He was not only cheerful, he was gay. Then we reached
the end of the town and the high road stretched before
us. There was no longer any possibility of losing the

way. I stopped the car and the boy jumped out.

'Bon voyage,' he said, with a smile, as we started off again.

I had rewarded him adequately, even generously I hope, for the service he had done me, but that is all I can say. The encounter was so unexpected, the boy's story so strange, that I had not time to bethink myself. When it was too late I wished that instead of a few pesetas I had given him enough to keep him for a month or two at least. I wished I had offered to take him on to Salamanca. I do not know what he would have done there, but he might have liked the adventure, and at all events I could have given him board and lodging for a while. For there, in flesh and blood, to-day was the picaroon of history. It was when he was fourteen that Agustin de Rojas ran away to Seville to be a soldier; it was when he was fourteen that Lazarillo de Tormes left his father's house to make his astonishing way in the world. Since then I have often, not without uneasiness, wondered what has happened to this little boy. I wonder if he has starved to death. I wonder if he has gone to gaol. (That would not matter so much, it would be part of the luck of the game). I wonder if the authorities got hold of him and sent him back to his own country. He was quick-witted, courageous and hardy. I have a feeling that he would find himself in no predicament that he could not wriggle out of. I have a hope that like those ancestors of his that he does not know, the careless picaroons of the Golden Age, he will go from master to master, now with good hap, now with bad, from one improbable adventure to another, light-fingered of course, keeping his head, with his bright alert eyes always on the watch to seize the passing chance and so make himself in the end master of the world whose only sense, so far as he can tell, is that it is there for him to exploit.

VI

I THINK it was George Borrow who said that the Spanish language was greater than its literature. The statement is true. The language is an instrument of strength and delicacy. It has a grandeur that gives ample opportunity for oratorical effect (an opportunity the Spanish authors did not neglect) and a concreteness that enables it to be written with exquisite simplicity. It has a succinctness that Latin hardly surpasses.

There was a young man who went to Granada. It was his first visit. On the night of his arrival, after dinner, too excited to stay in, he went down to the town. Here, because he was twenty-four and also perhaps a little because he thought the gesture suited to the occasion he had himself directed to a brothel. He picked out a girl of whom he could remember nothing afterwards but that she had large green eyes in a pallid face. He was struck by their colour, for it was that which the old Spanish poets and story-tellers were always giving to their heroines, and since it is a colour very seldom seen in Spain the commentators have opined that when the writers talked of green they meant something else. But here it was. When the girl stripped the young man was taken aback to see that she was still a child.

'You look very young to be in a place like this,' he said. 'How old are you?'

'Thirteen.'

'What made you come here?'

'Hambre,' she answered. 'Hunger.'

The young man suffered from a sensibility that was doubtless excessive. The tragic word stabbed him. Giving her money (he was poor and could not afford much) he told the girl to dress up again, and, all passion spent, slowly climbed up the hill and went to bed.

There is a passage in the autobiography (more or less true) of Alonso de Contreras, who began life as a scullion and ended it as a Knight of Malta, that has always seemed to me a masterpiece of narrative and an example of perfect style. Having at one period of his picturesque career married the well-to-do widow of a judge his suspicions were aroused that she was deceiving him with his most intimate friend. One morning he discovered them in one another's arms. 'Murieron,' he writes. 'They died.' With that one grim word he dismisses the matter and passes on to other things. That is proper writing.

There are innumerable idioms in Spanish; they give the language pungency. It makes an ampler and more complicated use of the subjunctive than most modern languages and so gets into its speech a great elegance.

We have pretty well lost the use of this mood in English and when we resort to it now it falls upon the ear affectedly; but it cannot, I think, be denied that it adds grace and distinction to a language. It is startling, and to anyone sensitive to such things charming, to hear a peasant in the course of conversation use with the accuracy of second nature the various forms of the subjunctive that the grammars give. Spanish has a harsher sound than Italian; it has not the euphonious monotony that makes that language somewhat fatiguing to listen to; it has a leaping, quick vivacity that forces the attention. It has nobility and deliberation. Every letter counts; every syllable has value. I like the story they tell of Charles V: he said that German was the best language in which to address horses, French to converse with statesmen, Italian to talk to women, English to call to birds; but that Spanish was the only language in which to address kings, princes and God.

It is with a certain dismay then that the student of Spanish literature grows little by little conscious of the fact that Spain has produced few works that are worthy of the instrument the writers had at their disposal. There is an engaging little story in the Spanish grammar. One day Louis XIV asked one of his courtiers:

'Do you know Spanish?'

'No, sire,' answered the other. 'But I will learn it.'

He set to work, for he thought it was the King's intention to appoint him ambassador to the Court of

Spain, and after a time said to the king:

'Sire, now I know Spanish.'

'Very good,' the king replied. 'Then you will be able to read Don Quixote in the original.'

That is a grand thing to be able to do It is an unforgettable experience; but it must be allowed that there is nothing else the foreigner can read (except perhaps a few poems by the enchanting Saint John of the Cross) that will leave him spiritually very much the richer. The fact is that the Spanish are not a highly intellectual people. They have added surprisingly little to the great stock of thought that forms the working material of our world. They have produced neither a philosopher nor a man of science of the first rank. Their best poetry, putting aside the ballads, was derived from Italy. Their great mystics took their ideas from Germany and the Low Countries. The most intelligent of them was St. John of the Cross. He was a rare poet, as lovely as Vaughan and as poignant as George Herbert. His prose reveals a character of appealing sweetness, a clear and discriminating brain, but a genius that was neither very profound nor very original.

I have a notion that the writers of Spain were hampered not only by a natural want of parts, but by a very singular circumstance. The great works of its literature were not produced by professional writers but by amateurs. They were soldiers broken by the wars, diplomatists in retirement, clerics who wanted to beguile their leisure, doctors and civil servants. The only important writer I can think of who made writing his profession is Lope de Vega. Cervantes, as we know, wrote when he was out of a job and it is pretty certain that if he had got one of the posts in America he applied for we should never have had Don Quixote. The professional writer is one who makes writing the main business of his life; therefore, unless he has some fortune, it must be also his means of livelihood; but whether he is paid by a sinecure in the customs, by a benefice or by royalties is of no consequence. In every occupation the professional is better than the amateur. No one would dream of denying this in any practical matter and it would be a great fool who employed an amateur plumber to repair a leak in a pipe. In music, sculpture and painting the amateur is rightly regarded with disdain. It is understood that to compose a piece of music or to carve a statue, a long apprenticeship and a cognizance of technique are needed. But because everyone learns to write well enough to put on paper in some sort of fashion what he wants to say, it is supposed that anyone can write a book. It is asserted that everyone has it in him to wrote one book. It may be so, but if by this is meant that everyone has it in him to write one good book, the assertion is false. The writer needs as complete a training as the practitioner of any other of the arts and the technique of writing yields to none of them in its difficulty. It is true that many professional writers write very badly, but many composers compose trivial and imitative music, many painters paint bad pictures. It is true also that sometimes an amateur writes a book better than many a professional. This is the stumbling-block of my argument.

The professional writer is confounded by this or that book written by someone who has never written before, or by someone who writes only as a diversion from other work, and because it has merit he is thought bound to admit that in writing the professional and the amateur are equal. But they who claim that Jane Austen is an example are in error, for to write was surely the main occupation of her life and the progress she made in the art sufficiently proves that she was a professional writer. Only her comfortable circumstances prevented her from pursuing it as a means of livelihood. It is, however, true that the amateur has some advantages that may give his work charm. The occasions of his life may provide him with a subject that is in itself interesting. He may have an attractive freshness. If his character is engaging or odd, his inexperience may allow him to reveal it so unaffectedly that his work has a quality of delight. Sincerity and a natural distinction sometimes enable him to string words together with clearness and elegance. But this is rare. To write simply is as difficult as to be good.

As a rule the amateur is rhetorical. He has an inordinate liking for picturesque words and high-flown phrases. At the back of his mind are all manner of literary tags and he brings them in under the impression that they look workmanlike. He cannot say a thing directly; he muffles it up in a periphrase. He uses two words when one will do; he never learns the art to blot. He does not know where to begin nor when to stop. He is the slave of every idea that enters his head so that he wanders from his subject with every fancy that strikes him. He is long-winded. I should say that the three essentials of good writing are lucidity, euphony and simplicity; and their importance is according to the order in which I have placed them. It is good that the reader should know exactly what you want to say and it is good that your words should fall pleasantly on the ear; a simple vocabulary is very desirable, but it is well to be prepared to sacrifice it if your meaning is not clear and you may without reproach choose an elaborate word rather than a plain one if its sound, in its place, is more delightful. Now it is very seldom that these three things come from a happy accident of nature; for the most part they are achieved by intensive training and assiduous labour. It is only by practice that the writer learns to stick to his point, which is the first and best rule of composition, and it is again only by practice that he learns how to present his theme with order, balance and succinctness. To do this, writing must be not only the main, but the only occupation, of his life. It is not often that the amateur will write a book that has the beauty of finish.

But the worst thing about the amateur is that he has no capacity to progress. He is wise if he writes but one book. This may have uncommon merit, but the chances are that anything else he writes will have very little. No country can have a great literature that has not had a number of writers who have been copiously productive. A writer is not made by one book, but by a body of work. It will not be of equal value; his books will be tentative while he is learning the technique and developing his powers; and if, as most writers do, for it is a healthy occupation, he lives too long, his later work will show the decline due to advancing years; but there will be a period during which he will bring forth what he had it in him to bring forth in the perfection of which he was capable. For talent is not something that is set and unchanging. Talent, I take leave to suggest, is made up of two things. It consists of a natural aptitude for creation, which to some degree is common to all young people. Innumerable youths have a facility for writing, they are prodigious letter-writers, they keep voluminous diaries; and if they have it to a considerable extent, but not something else, they become journalists, critics, professors of literature and so forth. The something else is an outlook on life peculiar to themselves. When these two are combined you have talent. This peculiarity of outlook will appeal to a certain number of people, either from its strangeness, which excites their interest, or because they share it; and then the writer will have readers and they will think him a devilish clever fellow. Sometimes there will be found a man who has this facility for writing to an extraordinary degree and to this joins an outlook on life which is not only peculiar to himself, but appeals to all men, and then he will be called a genius. The word is used carelessly nowadays; I should have said that such a one arises not more than two or three times in a century.

If this is what talent is it is plain that the professional writer has an advantage over the amateur. For the aptitude for writing can certainly be improved by study and practice, while that idiosyncrasy, which I think is the important part of talent, can be developed by the hazards and experiences of life. A writer has talent because he is himself, but in youth he is himself uneasily and with timidity. He only learns to look at the world characteristically when from indifference or obstinate courage he has freed himself of the current prejudices that on all sides surround him.

On the whole the defects you find in the Spanish writers are those you expect amateurs to have. They wrote as a pastime or because, having failed in their lawful avocations, they were short of money. Conceptism and gongorism, which corrupted Spanish literature for the best part of a century, are the frivolous amusements of dilettantes. Common sense was sacrificed to a striving for wit. Authors asked you to warm yourself at a display of fireworks and to make your dinner on a dish of larks' tongues. (Conceptism is the search for brilliant and futile conceits and gongorism expresses them with an obscure vocabulary in affected language and with forced antitheses. Conceptism is to the thought what gongorism is to the expression.) Spanish literature is of no great imaginative power, for the imagination is a faculty that is increased by exercise; it is not with the first caper that it reaches its utmost heights. It is a literature not of sustained force, but of brilliant beginnings. It is not easy to find in it works that keep a bold and decided line from start to finish. A greater knowledge is required, a larger experience and a more solid technique, to produce a complete work, with its various parts in due relation to the whole, than the Spanish authors often had. Perfection, we know, is not to be reached, but I think it has never been more completely missed than in Spain by writers with such gifts. Don Quixote is a very great work; it would be hard to find one of so much importance (and it is the only Spanish work that has a sure place in the literature of the world) that had so many glaring defects. I should not venture to speak of so celebrated a book, but for the fact I have noticed that pretty well all the references that are made to it in the literature of to-day are taken from incidents that occur in the first eight or ten chapters. I surmise from this that few people have read more. It is a pity, since the rest of the book contains many things that are worth attention. Cervantes, soldier, captive, tax-collector, jail-bird, place-hunter and maquereau, was the typical amateur. Don Quixote, as we know, was begun as a short story (a medium that had great vogue during the Golden Age) and it was the success it had when he read it to his friends that is said to have decided Cervantes to make it into a book. It is interspersed after the fashion of the day with short stories. They are very dull. The critics carped at them and in the second part, though still fantastic and absurd, they are brought more naturally into the body of the work. The wise-cracks of Sancho Panza, which at the beginning fall so naturally from his lips, are later piled on one another so extravagantly that they become tedious. Cervantes fell into the common error of the amateur who, when he gets hold of a good thing, harps upon it out of all reason. The device by which much of the action in the second part is carried on is very clumsy. Cervantes feigned that the first part had been published and read by many of the persons with whom the knight on his last journey came in contact. To my mind he has thus deprived the second part of all sincerity. The reader is no longer asked to believe what he reads. The last chapters are scamped. But the greatest blot, which must outrage the feelings of any sensitive person, is that Cervantes understood the character of his hero so little as to make him do something that it was impossible for him to do. He tells us that Don Quixote confessed on his death-bed that he had invented the account of his adventures in the Cave of Montesinos. Everyone knows that Don Quixote was incapable of saying anything that he did not think was true. When Cervantes made him admit a lie he maligned his hero and stultified himself.

It is unnecessary for me to say anything of the merits of Don Quixote. They shine like the sun at noon. Don Quixote is the most human and the most lovable character that the mind of man has invented. One cherishes him with a tenderness that, alas, one can seldom consistently feel in this difficult world for creatures of flesh and blood. The knight and his squire are immortal. There is one very good thing to be said of posterity, and this is that it turns a blind eye on the defects of greatness. Contemporary opinion is more concerned with the faults of a writer than with his excellence, but posterity takes him as a whole and very sensibly accepts the faults as the inevitable price that must be paid for the excellence.

But it is no business of mine to write a discourse on Spanish literature; if the reader finds what I have had occasion to say tedious, I beg him to forgive me; my only concern is with certain writers I have studied for a special purpose. I would only add that Spanish literature of course has many virtues. If I have pointed out that they are the virtues of amateurs it has been mainly with the didactic intention of emphasising (for

the good of my fellow-writers) that in literature, as in
other æsthetic occupations, you are more likely to
achieve art if you make a business of it. Spanish literature
has spontaneity. It has strangeness. It has a savour of the
soil. It represents very well those brutal, courageous, passionate, idealistic, earthy, humorous, cruel and humane
men who subjected a continent and discovered a world.

One would have thought that it would be the most
delightful thing possible to read the picaresque novels;
especially if one had not only the interest of the stories
and the various types that play their part in them, but
also the interest of looking for telling details on the
manners and customs of the day with the chance always
of hitting upon an incident here and there that (following
the example of many another writer) one could make
profitable use of. On the contrary it is in the main a
dreary business.

It is far from my purpose to instruct the reader, I have
quite enough to do to instruct myself, but I may state
in passing that the picaresque novel is one in which the
characters are taken from the dregs of society and in
which the hero lives on his wits. It is generally written
in the first person. The hero in the classic type of
the kind is a serving-man who goes from master to
master. This is obviously a very convenient way of
taking him through a variety of adventures and showing
a diversity of conditions. It is the most characteristic
form of Spanish literature. Its widespread influence was

peculiarly felt in England and but for its vogue the novels of Defoe, Fielding, Smollett and Charles Dickens would most likely be different from what they are. It is often said to have been invented in Spain and certainly no picaresque novels were more popular in Europe than the Spanish, but Spaniards have never so far as I know invented anything, and I should have thought students could trace the origins of the form without great difficulty back to the Golden Ass of Apuleius, the Satyricon of Petronius and the dialogues of Lucian. But this is of no great importance. It is the counterpart of the romances of chivalry, which as we know were for long inordinately enjoyed in Spain, and responds to that other side of the Spanish character, the mocking, realistic one, which so strangely exists cheek by jowl with the idealistic and mystical.

The best of these novels (barring Gil Blas, which was written by a Frenchman) is the shortest and the first. Its success established the form in the public favour. This is Lazarillo de Tormes. The historians of literature say that it was occasioned by the change in social conditions, the ruin of commerce, industry and agriculture, and the centralisation of power in the capital, which attracted to it adventurers of all kinds. But novels are not written for reasons of this sort now, at least not readable ones, and I very much doubt if they were in the sixteenth century. It never occurs to the critics that writers often write for fun. I should have thought the author, whether the monk Juan de Ortega or the retired diplomatist Diego de Mendoza, knowing his classics and being well acquainted with the Celestina of the Archpriest of Hita, thought it would be amusing to write the autobiography of a young scamp, and having got hold of a good idea, did what authors do in such a case, wrote it. He was a humorist and it gave him the opportunity to say many sharp things about monks and priests. The little book is no longer than Sterne's Sentimental Journey. It tells the birth and childhood of the picaroon and his sojourns with various masters, a blind beggar, a priest, a squire, a mendicant friar, a seller of indulgences, a chaplain and a policeman. It leaves him as town-crier and the complaisant husband of an archdeacon's mistress. The incidents follow so fast on one another that the reader is constantly entertained. In the squire whom Lazarillo served in Toledo the author was lucky enough to describe for the first time a type, the proud, hungry, dignified and melancholy gentleman, that, from its humour and pathos, went to the heart of his countrymen. It would be difficult to count the number of times this character has since then reappeared within the covers of a novel or on the stage of a theatre.

Lazarillo, wandering famished through the streets of Toledo, came upon a gentleman in sumptuous apparel who walked with measured steps. The gentleman looked at him.

'Boy, does thou want a master?'

'I would fain have a good master, sir.'

'Then follow me. God hath sent thee good fortune to meet with me, thou hast prayed well this day.'

The gentleman took him to a house, but the walls were naked, and there was not so much as a chair or a stool, nor a table, nor yet a coffer, so that you would have said it was uninhabited. And presently the gentleman asked him whether he had dined.

'No, sir, for it was not eight o'clock when I met with your mastership this morning.'

'Then,' said he, 'as early as it was, I had broken my fast, and whensoever I break my fast in the morning, I never eat again till it is night, therefore pass thou over the time as well as thou canst and we will make amends at supper.'

Taken aback, Lazarillo hid himself behind the door, where he drew some pieces of bread out of his bosom that he had been given in charity two days before. But the gentleman saw him.

'Come hither, boy,' he said. 'What does thou eat?'

He showed him the bread, and the gentleman took a piece.

'By my soul, methinks this bread is good and savorous,' he said.

No supper was forthcoming and next day, driven by hunger, Lazarillo went a-begging from door to door.

When he came home again with his spoils, not only bread but tripe and a neat's foot, he found his master awaiting him.

'I have tarried for thee to dinner,' he said, mildly, 'and because I could not see thee come I dined alone.'

The boy began to eat his victuals and his master eyed him hungrily. Whereupon the boy said:

'Sir, the good tools make the workman good, this bread hath good taste, and this neat's foot is so well sodden, and so cleanly dressed, that it is able with the savour of it only to entice any man to eat of it.'

'What is it, a neat's foot?'

'Yes, sir.'

'Now I promise thee it is the best morsel in the world, there is no pheasant that I would like so well.'

'I pray you, sir, prove of it better and see how you like it.'

The boy gave him the neat's foot, with two or three pieces of the whitest bread he had, whereupon the gentleman sat down beside him and began to eat like one that had great need, gnawing every one of those little bones better than any greyhound could have done for life.

He had land that, if it were in a better situation and had a great house on it, would be worth much money; and he had a dovecot that, had it not been in ruins, would yield him more than two hundred pigeons a year. These he had forsaken for matters that touched his honour. Had he not almost beaten a craftsman who on meeting him had greeted him with the words: 'Sir, God maintain your worship'? The proper way for a man of that condition to greet a knight or a gentleman was to say: 'I kiss your worship's hand'; and he would not suffer any man, unless it were the king, to say to him: 'Sir, God maintain you.' He was come to Toledo to serve some great nobleman. He was starving. But he remained dignified, kindly and courteous. He was bound to none but to God and to the Prince. He maintained his honour unsullied and that was the only refuge of an honest man.

In the morning when he rose he made clean his hose, his doublet and his cloak; Lazarillo gave him water for his hands; he combed his hair and taking his sword kissed the pommel.

'My boy,' he said, 'if thou knewest what a blade this is thou wouldst marvel; there is no gold that can buy it of me, for of as many as Antonio made he could never give such temper to any as he gave this.'

He drew it from the scabbard and tested the edge with his fingers.

'Seest thou it? I dare undertake to cut asunder with it a whole fleece of wool.'

Then putting up his sword, he hung it at his girdle and with leisurely gait strode out of the house. He held himself erect, casting the end of his cloak sometimes upon his shoulder and otherwhiles under his arm, with his right hand always on his side. He went up the street with such comely gesture and countenance that you would have judged him to be near kinsman to the High Constable of Spain. Who would have thought that such a noble gentleman had eaten nothing all yesterday but one piece of bread that his servant Lazarillo had kept in the chest of his bosom a day and a night? He went to a garden of the town over the water and dallied with personable women, devising and counterfeiting all kind of bravery, reciting more pleasant and sweet words than ever Ovid wrote. And when Lazarillo could beg nothing and his master had not a morsel to eat, still he would brave it out, walking at his accustomed stately pace, and when he came home stand at the door of his house and for his honour's sake pick his teeth with a straw to show to all men that he had richly dined.

Though hunger might gnaw his vitals despair could not subdue his courage. A gentleman and a man of honour he faced adversity without dismay. The Spanish, with a tear and a smile, have recognised in him a true Castilian. It was to such as he that they owed their greatness and their ruin. Even the scamp who served him loved him well. He pitied him for all that he saw him suffer and notwithstanding his fantastical pride was glad to have him for his master.

Tenderness like this is unique in the picaresque novels. They offer you but a monotonous recital of mean shifts, petty thieving and brutal jests. The most popular of them all was Guzman de Alfarache. Most of the critics describe it as a work of infinite tediousness; but I knew that my favourite Hazlitt greatly admired it; he praised it for the fine mixture of drollery and grave moralising. The witty and brilliant Jesuit Baltazar Gracian is said to have kept it constantly by his side both for its entertainment and its excellent style. I read it then with curiosity. Of the style a foreigner can only speak with diffidence, but even a foreigner can see that it is simple, unaffected and vivid. It has a coolness and discretion that you do not find in English till Dryden nearly a century later learnt it from the French. If good writing should be like the conversation of a well-bred man then it is obviously very good writing indeed. But no academic critic could exaggerate the tediousness of the matter. I do not think it is in human nature to read the whole work through. The hero is by turns a scullion, a porter, a gallant, a soldier, a beggar, page to a cardinal and pimp to an ambassador, a merchant, a student and finally a galley slave. Each of his adventures is followed by a long moral disquisition and strangely enough it is to these intolerable homilies that was due the book's enormous vogue with the readers of its own day. It is interspersed with short stories, of which one, that of Dorido and Clorinia, has a grim brutality that is rather engaging. Of course it is possible to skip the stories and the moralising and read only the adventures. They are very boring. It is all pilfering, card-sharping, beastly practical jokes and vulgar cunning. They show a lamentable poverty of invention. Nor do any of the many characters that are introduced live. This fault Guzman de Alfarache shares with the rest of the picaresque novels. They are written, as I said, in the first person, and experience has shown that it is almost impossible to make the teller of his own story distinct and palpable. Even Le Sage, though not a few of his subsidiary characters are sharply outlined, left Gil Blas himself a baseless fabric. Guzman is little more than a common sneak-thief. The resourceful Raffles would despise his paltry cheats and pettifogging robbery and Sherlock Holmes would never waste his time to bring such an insipid scoundrel to justice. Edgar Wallace is better than all the picaresque novelists put together. Not only are the crimes he deals with on a grander scale, but he shows a vivacity of invention, a power of suspense, a feeling for the picturesqueness of life, that none of them approached. It would not be so very surprising if the critics of the future neglected the serious novels of our day in favour of detective stories, and in the histories of literature pointed out the variety of Edgar Wallace's characters and the raciness of his conversations. This is what has happened with these Spanish writers; for while the picaresque novels were being written, novels of a more serious nature, with a definite claim to be works of art, were being written too, the Diana Enamorada of Gil Polo, the Galatea of Cervantes, the Arcadia of Lope de Vega, and heaven knows how many more. Of one of them the curate in Don Quixote said that it was one of the most foolish books that had ever been written and the critics with one accord have found them unreadable.

In the whole course of Guzman de Alfarache's career of roguery there is but one enterprise that can afford satisfaction to the disinterested admirer of crime. He was the bastard son of a bankrupt Genoese settled in Seville and on his first arrival at Genoa, a ragged boy, he claimed relationship with his father's brother. With the ingenuous notion, common to the crooks of all ages, that though he used his fellows ill, his fellows were bound to use him well, he was much affronted when his uncle would not acknowledge him. Eight years elapsed and he made up his mind to get even with him. Having got possession of a considerable sum of money in Milan he set out for Genoa. There he passed himself off as Don Juan de Guzman, a Sevillan of means and birth. His father's family not recognising in this fine gentleman the rapscallion whom they had once driven out of the city, were glad to accept him for the wealth they presumed him to have and the grand connections of which he boasted. He spent his time in feasting and the society of comely women. He was open-handed. In order to keep the rich young man among them they went so far as to offer him in marriage a damsel of no fortune but great quality. He played cards with his visitors, allowing them to win when he pleased, but keeping the balance well in his favour; for the accomplishment on which he most prided himself was his skill in so manipulating the cards that he could afford to be indifferent to the luck of the game. He had made friends with the captain of a galley and by spinning him an elaborate yarn about an affront that he had to avenge, which would entail his secret departure from Genoa, arranged with him for a passage to Spain. When the sailing date was settled he got to work. He transferred his own effects secretly to the galley and bought trunks which he filled with stones. Two of them he deposited with his uncle for safety, under the pretence that they contained plate of great value and jewels. Two others, to give his landlord confidence, he left at the inn. He had a couple of chains, one of gold and the other of copper, but identical in appearance, and by a neat trick he managed to get a cousin to lend him six hundred ducats on the false one under the impression that he held the real one as security. He announced his immediate marriage to the poor but noble young woman who had been proposed to him, whereupon his acquaintance showered presents on him so rich that he confesses he was almost ashamed to take them. These also he conveyed to the galley. He arranged a final game of cards at the end of which all his friends' money was in his own pocket, went on board and in the morning found himself well out at sea with his booty.

Since the people he robbed are shown as despicable as the trickster, the reader is left with the satisfaction, which no pity disturbs, of a confidence trick carried out with complete success.

It is a relief to turn from this dull book to the Life of Marcos de Obregon by Vicente Espinel. It was something new in the picaresque novel, for it was a romanticised autobiography. Espinel's life was in itself a picaresque novel and to write his book he had to do little more than narrate his own experiences. He was born in the wind-swept city of Ronda. His grandfather, a native of Santillana (the birthplace of Gil Blas) had taken part in the conquest of Granada and the Catholic Kings had made him a grant of land. Espinel learnt Latin grammar and the elements of music and at the age of twenty set out to pursue his studies at the University of Salamanca. After a residence of two years this was closed on account of the troubles occasioned by the trial of Luis de Leon, and he returned, for want of money travelling on foot, to his native town. Here relatives founded a chaplaincy of which they made him chaplain. It provided him with funds to return to Salamanca. He was a poet and a musician, and this enabled him to enter the society of the men of letters and the men of birth who who resided in the city. But the desire of fame made him once more abandon his studies. He enlisted in the fleet that was at that time being collected at Santander. Plague, however, broke out and the fleet was unable to sail. Espinel found his way to Valladolid, where he entered the service of the Count de Lemos. He grew tired of this peaceful life after four years and set off for Seville to join the expedion to Africa that resulted in the defeat and death of the romantic King Sebastian of Portugal. Fortunately he arrived too late.

For a year he earned his living in Seville by writing obscene verse and playing his guitar in taverns and brothels. Then he sailed for Italy. Landing on the island of Cabrera to get water for the ship he and his companions were captured by pirates, taken to Algiers and there sold in slavery to a renegade. He was put to row in a galley, and after various adventures the galley was captured by the Genoese; he was released and landed at Genoa. From here, provided with money and a horse, he made his way to Flanders, where he joined the army of Alexander Farnese and took part in the siege of Maestricht. He made friends with Don Hernando de Toledo and returned with him to Italy. Under his protection he resided there for three years, writing poetry and studying music; he visited the cities of that beautiful country and then, his health no longer what it was, his youth past, he began to think that a more peaceful life would befit him; he returned to Spain, was ordained a priest and settled down in Ronda to pass his declining years in respectable tranquillity. He published his poems and produced a translation of Horace's Ars Poetica. But Vicente Espinel was a man whose passions were music and the delightful art of conversation. In Ronda there was no one he could talk to. Its inhabitants were concerned with nothing but the weather and the crops. His verse grew melancholy. He complained that people spoke ill of him. Presently he betook himself to Madrid. Here through influence he obtained the profitable chaplaincy of the Royal Hospital at Ronda, but he had little intention of abandoning the capital and so named a substitute to perform the duties of his office. The authorities of Ronda complained and notwithstanding his protests a royal order forced him to fulfil his charge in person. He spent three unhappy years in Ronda. His fellow citizens reproached him, certainly with justice, for his bad behaviour and licentious life; and at last, appointing another substitute, he returned to Madrid. He graduated as master of arts at Alcalá and the Bishop of Plasencia made him his chaplain and master of his music. The salary was generous and he settled down for good in the capital.

He was famous. He added the fifth string to the guitar and his contemporaries ascribed to him the invention of a stanza which was called after him Espinela. (For those interested in such things I may state in passing that the pattern was as follows: a b b a a c c d d c.) He was the friend of Cervantes and Lope de Vega. He was a figure at literary gatherings. Authors submitted their works for his approval.

In this pleasing manner he passed the last twenty-five years of his life. In his foolish youth, he wrote, he had had few virtues and many vices; he had not always observed the laws of temperance; he had enjoyed the pleasures of the table and had looked deep into the wine cup; he had made many a joyful sacrifice on the altar of the Cypriote. In plain words he had liked good food and good wine and wenched whenever he got the chance. Remembering past delights and hoping, he says, that his experiences would serve as a lesson to others, he wrote the novel which is called Vida de Marcos de Obregon. It was first published in 1618 when its author had reached the respectable age of sixty-six.

His aim was didactic, but his moral reflections are on the whole brief, and he reproved sin with the indulgence of one who knew the world. He ascribed the vices of men to error of judgment. Marcos de Obregon is not a knave who narrates his rogueries with complacency, but an observer who takes life as it comes. He does not move only in the dregs of society, but consorts also with gentlemen, men of letters and musicians. You cannot resist the conclusion that Vicente Espinel was a charming, amiable, courageous and sensible man. He had wit and he enjoyed life.

There is one episode in this book that is really moving. When Espinel (for it is of himself he writes though he purports to write of Marcos de Obregon) was captured by the Genoese in the Algerian galley they took him for a renegade, handcuffed him, beat him with cudgels and told him that on arriving in Genoa he would be hanged. When they beat him, he cried: 'They say there's no wood in Genoa, there's quite enough for me.' Two musicians who were standing by heard his retort and laughed. He knew one of them very well, but was ashamed to discover himself. The admiral, however, gave orders that until they knew who he was, for he denied that he was the renegade they took him for, he should not be ill-treated. They took off his handcuffs. There was something of a storm in the Gulf of Lyons and when it was past the Admiral, Marcello Doria, ordered his musicians to sing to him. The first thing they sang was a song that Espinel himself had written and composed. The refrain was:

'El bien dudoso, el mal seguro y cierto.'

('The good is doubtful. The bad sure and certain.')

They sang the verses one after the other, and when they came to the refrain for the last time he could not contain himself.

'And yet this pain of mine continues,' he cried.

The singer, hearing what he said, looked at him. But he was short-sighted and Espinel in rags. His hardships, his privations, had so changed him that he was scarcely recognisable. Francisco de la Peña, for that was the singer's name, stared at him, and then, suddenly, unable to speak, his eyes wet with tears, took him in his arms. He addressed the admiral.

'Whom does your excellency think that we have with us?' he said.

'Whom?'

'The author of these verses and this melody and of much else that we have sung to your excellency.'

'What do you say? Call him.'

The admiral was shocked to see a man of whom he had heard so much in such a plight. He forthwith gave him decent clothes and showed him favour.

It is a pleasant example of that peripeteia and anagnorisis which Aristotle considered the most affecting things in tragedy.

There is one thing that strikes the diligent reader of the picaresque novels and that is the strange way in which the authors neglected the opportunities the times afforded them. For it was a period of great events. Cervantes was wounded at the battle of Lepanto, the greatest victory of the second Philip's reign. The Netherlands revolted and the Duke of Alba was sent to quell the rebels. Portugal was joined to the Spanish Empire. In America new realms were added to it. Drake singed the King of Spain's beard at Cadiz and the Armada sailed from Lisbon to set the Infanta Isabel on the throne of England. I cannot remember that any of this material is used even for an incident. If the Indies are referred to it is only because an adventurer has returned from them with a fortune and there is a chance of robbing him. Certain personages have been to the wars in Flanders or set out for them. I have not read a story in which you are told what they did there. One would have thought that the expulsion of the Moriscos with the cruelty and extortion that attended it would have given Solorzano, for instance, one of the later picaresque authors, a subject he could have made good use of. For all you can tell none of them took the smallest interest in the happenings of their time. They continued to relate the knaveries of innkeepers, the wiles of beggars and the thefts of scullions. It seems all very odd till you remember that Jane Austen, during the Napoleonic wars, was content to describe (heaven knows, with exquisite humour) the sentimental dalliance of honest gentlefolk, and that Henry James, who beheld the rise of the United States from a provincial community to a world power, exercised his extreme subtlety on the anæmic passions of the fashionable world. I do not blame this; I merely remark on it: it may be that it is by a sound instinct that the novelist turns his back on the occurrences that are significant to the welfare of his country and the progress of civilisation to dwell upon the humdrum affairs of common life. There has only been one Sir Walter Scott and only one Tolstoi. It is true that the Moorish pirates ravaged the coasts of Spain and that the country was bankrupt and oppressed: the inns were shocking, the innkeepers extortionate and you might very well be given a cat for your dinner when you had ordered a hare.

Nor can the modern reader of these novels fail to be surprised at the small part that is taken by sex. I do not know whether this was due to the fear of the Inquisition (which kept a sharp eye on literary productions) or to the natural healthiness of the Spaniards who looked upon copulation as a normal function of the human animal of no more (and no less) consequence than eating and drinking. The fact remains that the picaresque novels are uncommonly chaste. Now and then the roguish hero casts an amorous glance on a lady of the town, but he is cheated of his money and sent unsatisfied away. Even this is rare. More often the young man's thoughts turn to the well-dowered maiden or the rich widow. His raptures have a practical basis. In such of these books as have a heroine for protagonist a good many assaults are made on her virtue (the Spaniard then as now conceiving sensibly that the first thing to do with a comely wench was to put her to bed), but she cunningly eludes pursuit; she makes good use of the effect she has produced to rob her admirers of their money, but does not surrender the precious jewel of her virginity except under the blessing of the church. There is thus a certain amount, though little, of honest-to-God lechery, but there is no love. On this subject I shall have a little more to say presently.

For love you must go to the autobiographical frag-
ments which Agustin de Rojas inserted in his Diverting
Journey. And in the life of himself written by the soldier
Miguel de Castro, there is an account of his passion
for a courtesan at Naples, which, sordid though it is,
has the authentic thrill. It is not a romantic love that
he feels for the pretty trollop, but it is love all the
same, fierce, jealous, eager, a love for which he will
incur any danger and take any risk, a love capable even
of generosity and self-sacrifice. Incidentally the story
gives an unexpected and agreeable light on the relations
between soldiers and their officers, servants and masters.
For Miguel de Castro at this time was body-servant to
Don Francisco de Cañas, commander of the garrison.
Having discovered his servant's infatuation Don
Francisco, benevolently, though surely unreasonably,
sought by reproof and good advice to wean him from it.
But finding that notwithstanding his admonitions the
gallant spent all his nights with the harlot he had the
doors of the palace locked and the keys brought to his
own chamber. Miguel de Castro stole them. Then
he made him sleep in an inner chamber from which
he could only get by passing through the room in which
he himself slept. The lover found means to outwit
him. Finally in despair he sentenced him to a month's
imprisonment, thinking that thus he would put a stop
to the attachment that not only outraged his sense of
propriety, but jeopardised the soul of his unworthy

servant. This is how Miguel de Castro describes what followed:

'On issuing from the prison and chamber of my seclusion, it was not half an hour before I went forthwith to see the crocodile of my ignorance, the siren of my senses, the rock of Sisyphus on my shoulders, the wheel of Ixion of my torment; for there was the Wagoner's Rest of my sensibility, the hostelry of my faculties, the theatre of my delights, the idol of my sacrifices and the law of my faith.'

A lover can't say fairer than that.

VII

I MUST here remind the reader that I am making no attempt to give an exhaustive account of the Spanish, and their manners and customs, in the Golden Age. That would need a much greater erudition than I can pretend to. It would be a life's work. I have read with a special object in view and I have not concerned myself with what could be of no use to me. But I thought I could not deal properly with my hero's peregrinations unless I could get some idea of how people talked among one another. Judging from modern novels I surmised that the conversation in the romances of roguery was somewhat stylised. Naturalistic dialogue, indeed, is an invention of our own time. I thought I was more likely to find the racy speech of the average man in a conversational manual devised to enable English people to learn Spanish than in any work of fiction. In such a book, it seemed to me, the back-chat of common talk would be set down without literary flourishes; and I should hear, through the long course of time, the voice of a man addressing his wife, how servants spoke to one another in their master's absence and what a traveller said when he arrived at an inn.

I discovered a book with the following title page: Pleasant and Delightful Dialogues in Spanish and English, profitable to the learner, and not unpleasant to any other Reader. By John Minsheu Professor of languages in London. *Virescit vulnere virtus.* Imprinted at London, by Edm. Bollifant, 1599.

John Minsheu, it appears, was a lexicographer and he made his living as a teacher of languages. His name looks Catalan. I have wondered whether he was not a Spanish Jew who had sought asylum in our more tolerant country. He was poor. He managed to complete his lexicographical works by the help of generous patrons. To finish his Spanish dictionary he went to Cambridge where he found friends and subscribers. He likewise passed several months at Oxford, with his company of strangers and scholars, but that ancient seat of learning furnished him with no subscribers. He seems to have been a laborious student, lighting the candle for others, he says, and burning out himself. Ben Jonson, according to Drummond, described him as a rogue, but with exasperating brevity left it at that. He went into no details.

John Minsheu said no more than the truth when he described his dialogues as pleasant and delightful. They afford a lively picture of the times and besides the colloquial speech give a curious glimpse of everyday life. One who had studied them could find his way about the use and habit of the country with comfort. The banter is coarse and it is a trifle surprising to see what sort of things it was thought necessary for a learner to be able to talk of. But it was a less squeamish world than ours (at least that of the day before yesterday) and I do not suppose John Minsheu's crude words would have brought a blush to Queen Elizabeth's maiden cheek. In the dialogue that I am about to give, not only because it is entertaining, but also because it is instructive, I have, for the convenience of the reader, here and there rearranged the punctuation, but I have left the spelling untouched. I have thought it would save him from embarrassment in just the same way as it does when a bawdy word in an English book is given in French.

There are seven dialogues altogether, and this is the fourth 'between two friends, the one called Mora, the other Aquilar and a Muletier and a Woman Innkeeper: heere in are handled things pertaining to the way with very pleasant sayings, and gracious speeches.' I have slightly abbreviated it.

MORA: Ho, Peter, have you brought my mule?
PETER: Yea, sir, here is the Mohina . . . (a shee mule with a black face or mussell, alwaies having jadish tricks).
MORA: Mohina is never good.
PETER: Why, sir?
MORA: Bicause neither a mule with a blacke mussell,

nor a maide that hath passed the sea, nor a servant Peter (a knavish servant) in one's house, nor a neighbor abbot, nor a well at the dore, is ever good.

PETER: I promise your worship that she is better than that which dragged along the curate when he said, Dominus providebit.

MORA: Is she old?

PETER: I saw her not foaled, but I believe that hir dame was elder.

MORA: Doth she kicke?

PETER: She never gives one alone.

MORA: They are alwayes by couples. Doth shee travell well?

PETER: She never travels but shee leaves the way behind her.

MORA: She hath so good tricks in faith that I am in love with her.

PETER: One she hath above all, for she is a great astronomer.

MORA: How so?

PETER: She knowes better than a clocke when it is noone, and foorthwith she lookes for provender; and if they give her none, then she saies lunes and stirres not a foote from the place. (Lunes, meaning here the grunting voice of a mule or horse, but Lunes properly signifieth Mondaie.)

MORA: A good remedie for this to intreat her with the spurre.

PETER: She is most weak of memorie.

MORA: How?

PETER: Although you strike into her a hand's breath of the spurre, within two steps after she hath forgotten it.

MORA: Bring her, I care not, for Sancho hath met with his palfrey, and if she be a knavish jade I am as knavish a rider, and we shall understand one another by couples.

PETER: You travelling with her, with good heed, you may agree like the waxe and the weeke. But shee with one that is not aware of hir will play hir part like a fencer. (The waxe of the candle, and the weeke of the candle.)

MORA: Sit on the saddle, girde hir harde with the girts, put on the crouper and poitrell, make shorter these stirrups, for I will make agreement with hir.

PETER: I will put on newe stirrup leathers for more security.

MORA: Put on the bridle, make the bit fast, make shorter the headstall, looke if shee be well shod of all fower feete.

PETER: On the forefeete she hath good shooes and nailes; on the hinder feete she weares out hir owne hoofe. (With kicking.)

MORA: Put the cushion on the saddle and the portmanteau.

AQUILAR: How now, companion, shall we make an end that we may get hence to day?

MORA: What are you come already and a horsebacke?

AQUILAR: You tarrie longer in setting your selfe in order than a bride.

MORA: Is your mule gentle?

AQUILAR: As gentle as a lambe. Do you not see he beares a maile?

MORA: From the stilwater, God keepe me; from the raging, I will keepe my selfe.

AQUILAR: For your mule it is sufficient that she is a mule with a blacke muzzele.

MORA: You hardly know him whom you never saw, but in faith this mule hath taken degree in Zalamanca.

AQUILAR: In what arte?

MORA: In the arte of villanie, Bachelor of the kicking art, Licentiat of lawes in Innes, and doctor in Astrologie and the Mathematikes.

AQUILAR: For this cause shee looks alwaies towards heaven.

MORA: It is to contemplate the stars, planets and signes, and their courses.

AQUILAR: Let us go, for we have a long journey.

MORA: How many leagues do you thinke to travell to day?

AQUILAR: I would willingly go twelve.

MORA: Then, in the name of God, Peter, holde this stirrup.

AQUILAR: Friend, are you called Peter?

MORA: At your service, sir.

AQUILAR: Then God do no more mischiefe to Peter than that he knowes himselfe how to practise.

PETER: There is no cause why God give you health, sir.

AQUILAR: I know that men ought not to flout their friends.

MORA: One friend to another friend, a Cinche in the eie. (Chinche, a little round creature with many feete, in hot countries, breeding in beds, bites worse than a louse, and stinketh filthily.)

AQUILAR: I will not go to law with you, Peter, for that you know so much.

MORA: A rasher of bacon savers more.

PETER: A mulitter knowes one point more than the divell.

MORA: Why, what thinke you, what wants Peter to become a divell?

PETER: No more than a yeere's apprentiship and a flesh-hooke.

AQUILAR: Why a flesh-hooke?

PETER: To pull your worships out of the caulderne when you go thither.

MORA: We are not to go to hell.

PETER: You are not to go, but they are to carrie you
             thither.

MORA: Come behinde me therefore, evill spirit.
             Maledicte diabole.

AQUILAR: Friend Peter, of what is an old whore made
             of?

PETER: Of a young whore.

MORA: It is not made but of thy selfe and the herb
             dill, and of shitting eat thy fill, and of the
             dust of barn floore, or of the dust of which
             thou art thy selfe.

AQUILAR: I see him just over against me, and he hath
             shooes of packthred, and hee goes a foote.

MORA: Peter, harke what he saith unto thee. Doest
             thou not answere?

PETER: I heare not, for I am deafe of one of my
             chocke teeth.

MORA: What hath the master of fence of blowe or
             veine?

PETER: This wound hurts me not much, for it is
             given with the hand upward; but beware of
             the swash blow, for I will draw it with the
             hand downwards.

AQUILAR: Peter, I understand that you are hee which
             they called a plotter of knaveries?

PETER: Every one looke to himselfe, for I must
             plot something this journey.

AQUILAR: Peter, there commeth a traveller, bestowe a quip on him.

PETER: Holo, brother, which way go they?

TRAVELLER: Whither?

PETER: To the house of the queane thy mother.

AQUILAR: Good in faith. Another to his companion which remaines behind.

PETER: Ho, sir, is the mule yours?

TRAVELLER: What mule?

PETER: That whose arse kisse you.

AQUILAR: This gentleman which goeth so boldly, let him not passe without his flout.

PETER: Ho, sir, goes your worship to London?

TRAVELLER: Yea, I go for that you saie it.

PETER: Then a turd for him that goeth to London.

TRAVELLER: Oh, how proper a man were Peter, if he were washed and painted.

PETER: Nay, after I am washed I am worth nothing.

AQUILAR: How far have we journeyed, Peter?

PETER: I never turne to looke backe, because I would not be as Lot's wife.

AQUILAR: How far have we from hence to the next towne?

PETER: A league and a turd.

MORA: The league we will goe, the other thou shalt passe.

AQUILAR: That we may passe over this journey without wearisomnes, tell us a tale, Peter.

PETER: For my part, I would tell money with a better will.

AQUILAR: Not so, but some chaunce that hath fallen out to thee on these waies.

PETER: Then I will tell you one which happened unto me the last voyage I came this way with a gentleman.

MORA: Let it not be too long, for I will sleepe.

PETER: If you sleepe, the she mule will be carefull to wake you.

MORA: You have raised a thousand false testimonies against her. Behold how well she travelleth, and how well she goeth.

PETER: By the frying you shall see.

AQUILAR: Well, let us leave this. Forward with the tale.

PETER: A little while since I came this way with one of the greatest babblers that I knew in my life. And as much prating and lying are neere of kinne, hee tolde the most horrible lies that could be imagined.

MORA: Of one thing I woonder, Peter.

PETER: What is it?

MORA: How thou couldest endure so long time with thy competitor in thine owne facultie?

AQUILAR: Yea, for he is thy enimie which is of thy owne profession.

PETER: It is true. For many times I would leave him

for this cause, and did tel him that I would not travell no more with him, because he was infected with my disease and did not suffer me to take up a tricke.

AQUILAR: And what ansere made he to this?

PETER: Foorthwith he promised me with an oath that he woulde hold his peace all one journey, that I might speake.

AQUILAR: And did he performe it?

PETER: It was impossible for him to have power to accomplish it as for your worship to digest this asse's haire which you have eaten.

MORA: Companion, you are paid home for your labour.

AQUILAR: You mistake, Peter. I see you dimne sighted by reason of cloudes.

PETER: Rather wish I you blinde than that I see ill.

AQUILAR: Nay rather, that I may have my sight to see you an Archbishop with a miter of seven hand bredth's high. (i.e. Caroça, which is a high hat of paper set on the head of a bawde, riding on an asse thorow the streetes for a punishment.)

PETER: Nay, not so, but that I might also see you eat the shittings of your mule.

AQUILAR: I cast thee a bone, with his yong one to gnawe upon. Thy wife makes thee a hart, and they call thee cuckolde every one.

PETER: I cast the bone to gnaw upon at sea. Thy teeth fall out, and thy water hold in.

MORA: Let us spurre on, companion, for it waxeth late.

AQUILAR: What is it a clocke, Peter?

PETER: Just the same as it was yesterday at this time.

AQUILAR: This could my mule tell me if she coulde speak?

PETER: Am I a clocke that you aske me what it is a clocke?

AQUILAR: At least thou art a clapper, which is all one.

PETER: And if I do strike where shall I hit?

AQUILAR: Upon the head of the buggerer thy father.

PETER: Your head is neere unto me, and it will sound well seeing it is hollow.

MORA: Your mule doth go a swift easie pase.

AQUILAR: And yours ambles well.

MORA: And if she did not change it sometimes into a trot, which seemes like the trot of hir dam.

AQUILAR: Let us go into this Inne to baite and eate a little.

PETER: What, one bit and no more? I thinke to eate more than a hundred.

MORA: Can you not passe one daie, Peter, without eating?

PETER: By God our master, as the Biskaine saith, the bellie carrieth the feete and not the feete the bellie. (A Biskaine travelling a foote fainte for want of food, filled his belly, afterward went lustily, and said, the belly carrieth the feete, and not the feete the belly.)

AQUILAR: I also say that bread and wine are travellers, and not the lustie frolike youth. (The lustie youth without eating or drinking must needs faint, and give him that, although he be faint he goeth forward.)

PETER: Peace be in this house. Who is here hostesse?

HOSTESS: Who is there? Who cals?

PETER: Have you lodging, mistris?

HOSTESS: Yes, Sir, come in and be very welcome, for all good entertainment is here to be had.

PETER: What shall we have to dinner?

HOSTESS: There are conies, there are partridges, there are chickens, hennes, geese, ducks; there is mutton, there is beefe, kid, and hogs' inwards.

PETER: Well saide I that in your house there could not want hog's flesh.

HOSTESS: Nor in your house shall there want a knave while you are within.

PETER: No, in truth, mistris, but they told me that a while agoe you and cleanliness had been at bate.

I

HOSTESS: And they told me that you had banished shamefastnes from your house.

MORA: I am glad, Peter, that thou haste mette with that thou haddest need of.

PETER: And also she hath need of me.

HOSTESS: I have need of him truly, if it be but to put him in Peralvillo to shoote twelve arrowes at him with the mistris; I know not for what els? (Mistris, that arrow which hitteth on the hart.)

PETER: Now, mistris, let us saaie no more. Holde your peace and let us be still, for we have a quip a peece.

HOSTESS: Go to, make an end, babbler in graine, and demand that you have need of.

PETER: Give me haie and straw and provender for the mules.

HOSTESS: How much will you have?

PETER: Two sieves full of haie and a peck of barley.

HOSTESS: It is very little for three beastes.

PETER: Heere are no more than two; which is the other?

HOSTESS: The other are you, and more devouring than the other two.

PETER: If I be more, it is not of straw nor barley, for it is very hard of digestion.

HOSTESS: Harder is a cudgell, and yet it useth to soften the ribs of a knave.

MORA: It is well, passe no further forward, mistresse hostesse. How far doe they count it from hence to the citie?

HOSTESS: Sir, five leagues.

MORA: May we ride them betwixt this and night?

HOSTESS: As you shal hasten.

MORA: Is there any river in the way, or any evill passage?

HOSTESS: Which way soever you goe, there is a league of evill waie.

MORA: Is there any place *herrar*. (To misse or erre. Also to shoe a horse or mule.)

HOSTESS.   The way, no, sir, the mules, yes, sir; a thousand passages where you may erre.

MORA: If they be errors for love they are worthie to be pardoned.

AQUILAR: Mistresse hostesse, whose is this inne?

HOSTESS: A gentleman of the citie.

AQUILAR: How much do you pay for the hire of it by the yeere?

HOSTESS: More than it is worth. Five hundred ducats.

MORA: By this meanes they had neede good skill to steale to get out their charge.

PETER: That skill wants not; a cat for hare flesh, the flesh of a mule for beefe, wine mixed with water; all goes in this manner.

HOSTESS: God send the knave an ill Easter and an ill

Midsommer. When have you seene this in my inne?

PETER: I have not seene, but I have tasted it.

HOSTESS: You lie like a knave. There was never any such matter.

PETER: Hostesse, we are upon the reckoning now, let us not give the devill his dinner. (Let us not braule and fall out, and so go to law upon words and so make the divell dine.) Come hither, doe you not remember the other daie, when I came this way with a gentleman which requested you to give him a peace of meate, of that which you had given him the day before when he passed this waie; bicause, he said, it liked his taste very well. The which the little childe hearing, saide, it would be deare flesh unto us, if every day there shoulde die a nagge.

HOSTESS: It is true there was a nagge which died, but hee was so fat and so faire that hee was better than beefe.

MORA: Misstresse hostesse, although he might be more fine, give us not of that nowe.

HOSTESS: No, sir, for he is already made an end of. What, think you it could last till now?

MORA: Let us see the wine that is so good.

HOSTESS: The wine is such that it is sufficient to bring a man to heaven that shall use to drinke it.

PETER: What now, Mistresse, is it not ynough to be a keeper of an Inne, except you be a heretike too?

HOSTESS: That which I say is true and I will proove it, that good wine carrieth men up to heaven.

MORA: How so ?

HOSTESS: Good wine makes good blood, good blood doth engender good condition, good condition doth ende in good works, good works carrie men to heaven.

MORA: She hath proved her intent very sufficiently.

AQUILAR: But this cannot be verified in this wine.

HOSTESS: Why?

AQUILAR: Because this seemes rather vinegar and water.

HOSTESS: Water! By the life of my soule it hath no more water in it then he from above put in it.

MORA: God never came to put water into wine, but without water he created it.

PETER: Well, you understand not the matter a right. He from above is hir husband, which is in the top of the house, and from thence puts water into the wine with a long tunnell.

AQUILAR: I will die and live with thee, Peter, for thou knowest fashions.

MORA: I understoode that she had called God him that was from above.

AQUILAR: In everything there is deceit.

PETER: Except it be in an old garment.

HOSTESS: Truely they have reason, for the worlde is very badde. For this cause have my husbande and I withdrawen our selves into this Inne to make an end in good life.

MORA: Call you this a good life, hostesse?

PETER: Yea, sir, for that of Sodom and Gomorra was woorse.

HOSTESS: Do you not thinke that it is a goode life to be made Hermites in this desart? What did the fathers in the wilderness more then this?

PETER: And so holie that of pure almes, of as many as passe they take away that they carrie.

HOSTESS: Take away, God forbid. Receive that they give us with curtesie, that we doe.

PETER: Thus it is they call the picklocke curtesie with which they open the mailes.

HOSTESS: The divell brought this servant to my house. Get thee hence in the divels name, thou spirit of contradiction.

PETER: My gossips cannot abide me, because I speake truth unto them truely.

MORA: Now, Peter, reckon with the hostesse and let us begone hence, for it is late.

PETER: Hostesse, what is owing in the whole?

HOSTESS: Tarrie a little, I will reckon. Two of straw, and of straw two, three of barley, five of wine, one of flesh, and two of bacon; ten shillings in the whole.

126

PETER: The reckoning made, the mule dead, serving man get your way a foote. Why, the mistresse hostesse will give me pap. Doth she not knowe that when she was borne, then did I eat bread with a hard crust? Tarrie, i'le make my reckoning.

HOSTESS: Make it; let us see.

PETER: Three and two are five, two of sack and three of wine somewhat blacke, and other three of the hurdes of flaxe and pitch, one of the pot, and two of the nowle (the hinder part of the head) and a half of the chibbowle. They are eight in the whole.

HOSTESS: What, with a mischiefe to you, paie mee heere. If not, by my father's soule i'le put out thine eies.

PETER: The cat hath cast off the garment of hypocrisie. Mistris Hermite, have patience and be not so covetous.

HOSTESS: Do not reckon up mortuaries unto me, but paie me. If not, I will pull off the haires of thy beard one by one.

MORA: Give that which the hostesse doth require, Peter, and braul not with her.

PETER: In a ship loaden with silver there is not enough to content hir.

HOSTESS: I require nothing but my right. Pay me, brother, and leave of words.

PETER: So saith the chattering pie. Holde, mistres, see heere six shillings. Three of them be much good doe it you with them, and the other three the divell choake you with them.

HOSTESS: Not so, but the one three are of welcome unto me, and the other three the divell go with thee.

PETER: Cursinges of old whoores are praiers of health.

MORA: God be with you, mistres Hostesse.

HOSTESS: God conduct your worships. Heere is this poore Inne; for as often as you shall come this way I entreate you to use it at your command.

PETER: Aunt, you do it upon a good sheafe of strawe.

HOSTESS: No, but onely for your faire lookes, sir.

PETER: Aunt, God be with you and make you a good hermite.

HOSTESS: Farewell, sonne, and God make thee better than that thou art.

VIII

IT would be absurd to suppose that one could
acquire from the picaresque novels more than a
partial knowledge of the behaviour, the ways of
thought and the sensibility, of the Spanish in the
Golden Age. They present but one side of the picture.
For another you must go to the drama, which at
no time and in no country has flourished so luxuriantly
as in Spain during the hundred years that ended with
Calderon's death. Now, the drama is a popular art and
in order to succeed a play must reflect the temper of
the age. A play is a close collaboration between the
author, the actors and the audience, and the audience
cannot play their part unless they can share and share
alike in the author's conception. The sentiments that
he sets before them must be those with which they are
in sympathy. He must feel as they feel and his morality
must be the same as theirs. Sometimes he expresses
sentiments and a morality that his audience have felt,
but from timidity or obtuseness have refused to put
into words; and then he is admiringly described as a
dramatist of ideas. The revolt of Nora came as a shock
to the world of her day, but the notion would have

seemed preposterous (and so the play would have failed) unless there had been an obscure, but deep-seated feeling among the spectators that woman had a right to her own personality. Thus by reading the drama of a period you can get a very good impression of what men and women thought on the great issues that influenced their lives.

But if the drama presents an adequate picture of the way men think and feel, contrariwise it influences their thoughts and feelings. It gives voice to the inclinations that they have repressed and by the vividness of its appeal enables them to carry into action the promptings of their hearts. The contagiousness of the emotions it arouses, the man to man address, give it a power incomparably greater than that of fiction. Far more wives left their husbands because Nora slammed the door in Torvald Helmer's face than ever men shot themselves because Werther suffered from the melancholia of the age. Though it must be admitted that suicide is a drastic and often painful affair. The dramatist not only represents the persons of his period, but by giving to their instinctive tendencies living shapes forms them after the pattern he has devised. So Mr. Coward not only portrayed the querulous frivolity of the decade that followed the Great War, but created a generation of querulously frivolous people. It is owing to this power that the playwright wields, that the church has always, and it may be with wisdom, looked upon the drama askance.

Now when you come to study the Spanish theatre from this point of view you make some very interesting discoveries. The field is enormous and I do not suppose even the most industrious student has completely covered it. Lope de Vega alone wrote as many plays as all the Elizabethan and Jacobean dramatists put together. He is said to have written two thousand two hundred. Nearly five hundred of these are extant. I have read twenty-four. It may seem impertinent to speak of a writer of whose work you claim to know but a fragment. I remember the story of Mr. Page, the publisher, who refused a certain novel that was sent him; the author then wrote an indignant letter telling him that she had stuck together two pages and since, when the novel was returned to her they were still stuck, it proved conclusively that he had not read her manuscript. 'Madam,' replied Mr. Page, 'it is not necessary to eat a whole egg to know that it is bad.'

For my part I have read with pleasure the twenty-four plays of Lope de Vega that have come my way, but I find in myself no overwhelming desire to read more. His fertility was of course amazing and fertility is a quality to be praised in an author. It denotes physical energy, a gift a writer can as little do without as a tennis player, vitality, power of invention and variety of interest, which may from time to time create a master-piece. I do not believe in your constipated geniuses. Lope de Vega said he had written twenty sheets every day of his life and more than a hundred comedies in twenty-four hours apiece. His contemporaries called him the Phœnix of Wits and Cervantes described him as a Prodigy of Nature. The reader (if he knows anything about men of letters) will, however, not be surprised to learn that there was no love lost between the two greatest authors of their time; and Lope, writing a chatty letter to a friend, remarked that there was no one so stupid as to praise Don Quixote. Lope's first acted play was written when he was twelve and for hard on fifty years he was supreme in the theatre. When the younger generation came knocking at the door he firmly put his foot against it. He had a small pension from the king and as a retainer of the great house of Manrique enjoyed the emoluments of a chaplaincy at Avila; but his main source of livelihood was his pen. The managers paid fifty ducats for a play. A ducat was worth five shillings, but so far as I can make out its purchasing power was about equal to that of a pound. Since this does not mean very much I have had the curiosity to note the relative prices that were paid for certain commodities. According to the contriver in Cervantes' Coloquio de Cipión y Berganza a man could live on a real and a half a day, and there were eleven reals in a ducat. From La Gitanilla I gather then ten ducats was a good price to pay for a donkey; fifty, as I have just said, for a three-act play; and when Cervantes was rescued from slavery in Algiers his ransom was five hundred. On the other hand when a middle-aged gentleman desired to be rid of Cervantes' daughter, who had been living under his protection, he had to provide her with a house and two thousand ducats. From this it is evidènt that a play was worth ten times as much as a donkey and a man of genius fifty times; but a maiden's innocence was worth more than four times as much as a man of genius. The price of a virtuous woman, as we know, is far above rubies.

Though certain critics carped (as critics will) because they thought that Lope did not pay sufficient respect to the precepts of antiquity, the public acclaimed him with a united voice. He was a popular dramatist. In that fortunate age this was not a term of reproach and Lope was thought highly of not only by the vulgar, but by the great, the good and the intelligent. Though from time to time (as authors will) he spoke bitterly of the public it was their suffrage he sought. 'If anyone should cavil at my plays,' he said, 'and think that I wrote them for fame, undeceive him and tell him that I wrote them for money.' He wrote to please. He was one of the few professional writers of his day and he had the professional writer's merits: he wasted no time on exposing his subject; incident followed incident, if not always with probability, generally with dramatic effect; his language was easy and natural, his dialogue pointed and quick. The necessity of getting through within a certain time and the greater necessity of holding the attention of an audience saved him from the two defects most common to Spanish literature, diffuseness and digression. Critics nowadays complain that the ending of his plays is hurried and it is true that in the study the knots seem to be cut rather than untied. He was an improviser, and with the improviser it is always the same thing: his theme and his beginning, which he owes to his native inspiration, are for the most part brilliant; but when his inspiration fails him he has no solid sense of construction on which to fall back nor the energy of mind to enable him by the exercise of reason to bring his work to a logical conclusion. But I am not sure if these scamped endings of Lope's were offensive in performance. He knew that when you have interested your public in the presentation of your subject and held them, by the display of unexpected or thrilling events, during its development, when the end is in sight you had better come to it as quickly as possible. The audience are done with you and so long as they can get out of the theatre speedily do not care much what means you use to give them their liberty. They are quick to see the upshot and easily bored if a sense of propriety induces you to gather all your threads together into a single pattern. They will take an astonishing amount for granted. The wise author brings down his curtain while his audience are still under the spell.

In the intolerable La Arcadia Lope makes one of his

characters say: 'Not only must the poet know all the sciences, or at least their elements, but he must have the greatest experience of all things that happen on land or sea . . . he must know as well the habit and the way of life, and the customs of all manner of people; and finally all those things of which they speak, treat and have their being . . .' It is an ideal at which none must more deliberately aim than the dramatist. Certainly Lope de Vega put himself in the way of gaining the experience that would be useful to him. His life, a long story of romantic adventures, violent passions and domestic virtue, reads like one of his own cape and sword plays. His first notable love affair was with the daughter of one actor and the wife of another. When she abandoned him for a more opulent admirer he revenged himself by writing scurrilous verses about her family. He was arrested, brought to trial and on pain of death exiled from Madrid. But in a short time he returned and ran away with Isabel de Urbina, whose father was King-at-Arms. He married her and immediately set sail in the Great Armada. He used the paper on which he had written verses to the fickle actress as gunwads. He saw his brother killed by his side. His wife died and three years later he married the daughter of a pork-butcher. In the interval he was prosecuted for his relations with a certain Antonia Trillo and fell in love with an actress called Micaela de Lujan. He had children by his wife and children by his mistress. By a happy coincidence each was brought to bed of a son, one only a few months after the other, and he proudly called them Lope Felix and Carlos Felix respectively. The pork-butcher's daughter died in childbirth about the middle of August in 1613 and in September Lope in the retinue of Philip III went to Segovia. He lived with the actress Jeronima de Burgos: 'Here I have seen the lords prowling around my house,' he writes; 'the gallants come, but with less money than we needed.' It looks as if the Phœnix of the Age was not above a bit of pimping when the occasion arose. At the beginning of the following year, being then a little over fifty, he determined to enter the priesthood and in March 1614 was ordained. His fertility did not abandon him, for he had two children by Marta de Nevares Santoyo, whom he celebrated as Amarilis in an eclogue, and continued to write plays, a great deal of poetry and some prose. He was a conscientious priest. He belonged to a pious fraternity that buried poor clerics, clothed the naked and assisted the needy; and as a familiar of the Inquisition he presided over the burning of a heretic monk. He performed these duties with Christian charity. He had an oratory in his modest house and spent there much time in prayer. He scourged himself so that the walls of his room were spattered with blood. Fray Francisco de Peralta in the sermon he preached at his funeral related that once a man came to his house and challenged him to a duel.

'Let us go outside,' he cried, drawing his sword.

'Let us go,' answered Lope, slowly putting on his cloak, 'I to the altar to say mass, and your worship to assist me.'

When he was buried, a great throng following, the funeral procession went out of the direct path so that it might pass by the convent of the Trinitarian nuns where his bastard daughter had taken the vows.

Though Lope de Vega wrote plays of all kinds, romantic, historical, pastoral and religious, his fame rests chiefly on the comedies of intrigue known as cape and sword. These present a vivid and varied picture of life as it may have been led during the Golden Age. His plays can be read with interest; a warmer feeling than that, they can now excite in few. With all his fluency, profuse invention, eye for dramatic effect and nimble sense of life's multifarious scene, he had a commonplace mind. He was a good-natured normal, sensual man. In fact he was exactly what a dramatist should be if he is to have success. His personality was of no great importance. His characterisation is thin and there is not one of his noble, passionate heroes that can be distinguished from another. Sometimes his women have the rudiments of individuality and occasionally show a trace of sardonic humour. His men never. His heroines know what they want, a man, and have no hesitation in using every means at hand to get him. Lope's great subject matter is love, love at first

K

sight, of a devastating kind, which stops at nothing
to obtain its satisfaction; but a reputable love for the
most part, whose end is marriage: the great lord may
have no intention of fulfilling his promises, but his lady
will not admit him to her bed till he has made them.
And oddly enough it is a love that ceases as suddenly
as it arose when marriage is out of the question. So,
in Lo Cierto por lo Dudoso, Don Pedro, the king, is
enamoured of Doña Juana and when she tells him that
his brother, Don Enrique, has kissed her, in his fury
gives orders that he shall be killed; but no sooner does
he discover that Doña Juana and Don Enrique are
already married than his passion is immediately extin-
guished and he gives the pair his blessing. And in
another play, called Por la Puente, Juana, when a
nobleman gets the object of his affections alone on an
island in the Tagus she has but to tell him (in a hundred
and fifty lines) the story of her life for him to hand
her over to her affianced husband. Indeed he carries
his generosity so far as to provide her with a dowry.

It would be impertinent in a foreigner to attempt to
judge the merit of Lope's verse. I can recognise its ease
and grace. It is not often monotonous. In his frequent
scenes of rapid, broken dialogue he manages with uncommon skill to preserve the pattern. But I do not feel
anywhere the ring of true poetry. When he indulges
in general reflections he is platitudinous and it requires
a good deal of patience to read him when he breaks into

a purple passage. You wish then that the Renaissance had never rediscovered Antiquity so that you might have been spared these tedious allusions to the gods of Greece and the iron-hearted heroes of Rome. And there must be few who can suffer gladly the carnations of so many ladies' cheeks, the pearls of their teeth, the snow of their brow and the marble of their hands.

But what a happy state of affairs when an audience was ravished by verse for its own sake! Of course few people could read and their ears were more sensitive than ours. Books were scarce; the reader will remember that in the castle of so respectable a family as the Loyolas there were but two books. I think it is not merely patriotic bias that makes me believe that in an English country house of the same standing you would find to-day not only the Bible and the works of Shakespeare, but also a good many bound volumes of Punch and Ruff's Guide to the Turf. I know little of the mysteries of versification and I must accept from the histories of literature the fact that Lope de Vega was a master of all its forms. His plays, to tell the truth, can be best appreciated if you look upon them as operatic 'books' in which verse takes the place of music. He will write a bravura passage in which three persons, for instance, embroider upon an idea, each one ending his speech with the same refrain, so that you can almost hear the burst of applause that greets the ingenuity. Sometimes a character will present a theme in four lines and then enlarge upon it in stanzas each of which ends with one of the four lines. It is as much a set aria as La Donna è mobile. In one of his plays that I have read all the soliloquies are cast in sonnet form. It gives a formal distinction that must have been very grateful to an audience sensible to such elegancies. It further gives the soliloquies a pleasing brevity. I have read somewhere that the courtiers of Philip III used to amuse themselves by carrying on among themselves conversations in verse. It was an amiable accomplishment.

Theatres were originally the yards of houses. At the back was the stage and persons of quality viewed the play from the windows of the houses built round the yard. In the yard stood the populace. Raised benches surrounded it for those who could afford to pay for seats, and the women sat in a gallery, called the cazuela or stew-pan, which had a separate entrance and into which men were not admitted. Nevertheless it was hard to keep them out, and I have read that Bernardo de Soto having got in raised the petticoats and touched the legs of the women who were watching the play, by which great scandal was occasioned. So keen was the demand for seats that sometimes windows and benches were left as heirlooms. The public that stood in the pit, students, artisans and ruffians, was most disorderly. As many of them as could got in without paying and there were frequent brawls at the door as they tried to force their way past the doorkeeper who took the entrance money. Once in they waited noisily. Itinerant vendors walked about crying their wares (as they still do at bull-fights), selling fruit and candy; someone would throw down money in a handkerchief and the vendor, wrapping up in it what was wanted, would throw it back. Now and then a spectator would be tapped on the shoulder and asked if he would pay for a dozen oranges for a woman he had ogled in the stew-pan. Performances began at two in winter and at three in summer. They were given by the light of day and at first under the open sky so that a downpour of rain cut the play short and the money was returned. At the appointed hour, more or less, the musicians appeared, with guitars and harps, and sang a ballad. After this a member of the company came on the stage and recited a monologue, called a loa, which was designed to put the spectators in good humour. Then the first act of the play was given. It proceeded in so great an uproar that the words could often not be heard. When the public were displeased they broke into shrill whistles, cat-calls and scurrilous abuse. The women in the stew-pan were as vociferous as the men in the pit. But when they were moved by a noble sentiment or charmed by an adroit piece of versification they shouted Victor, Victor! To prevent the audience from being bored a short, often topical, farce followed the first act.

This was called an entremes. It was accompanied by music and ended with a dance. Then came the second act, another entremes, and the last act. But the public had a passion for short pieces called jacaras, which were roistering ballads in thieves' slang, and the mob clamoured for them at every interval. A final dance brought the proceedings to a close. The audience surely got their money's worth.

It is plain from these interruptions how little they cared to preserve the illusion of reality. Each act was almost a self-subsistent part of the general entertainment. The audience were not, one imagines, expected to enter into the emotions of the characters represented, but rather with cool minds to watch them. So they were able to give more attention to the ingenuity of the intrigue and the elegance, the variety and the appositeness of the language. Thus there was small reason why improbability and incoherence should incommode them. So long as a situation was effective they were not such fools as to ask how it had been come by.

I should like to give some description of one of Lope's plays, but it so happens that the play that I find most interesting was not written by him at all. It is called La Estrella de Sevilla and is printed in all the editions of his works. The experts however have shown (I do not know how, for I have not read their remarks) that Lope did not write it, and it remains of unknown authorship. Still, it has so many of his characteristics, it is so typical of the drama of the period, its characters and their motives conform so well with the prepossessions of the Spaniards of that day, that it does not matter who wrote it. It is an interesting piece, and I should think would act uncommonly well.

Don Sancho the Brave, King of Castile, makes a state entry into Seville and among the crowd who watch his progress catches sight of a most lovely young woman seated at her window. In the Spanish way he falls violently in love with her. She is known as the Star of Seville. Her name is Estrella, and this is very unfortunate, for it gives the various characters in the play an opportunity, which they seize with one accord, to be abundantly poetic. They play upon the name in harmonious numbers and show their wit in all manner of conceits. Even the heroine, when catastrophe befalls her, bewails her fate with every possible reference to her pretty name. She is the sister of a brave and gallant gentleman, Busto Tavera by name. The king is determined to gratify his desire that very night. His confidant suggests that Tavera should be granted favours and the king, sending for him, appoints him Commander of the troops on the frontier. When Tavera declines the honour he makes him a gentleman in waiting at his court. He declares besides that he will marry Estrella according to her station.

Now Estrella loves, and is loved by, a gentleman of Seville, Don Sancho Ortiz, and their marriage has been arranged. When Tavera, suspicious because the king has thus favoured him, tells them that his royal master has decided to dispose of her himself, and dower her, they are dismayed. Night comes and the king, disguised, is wandering about Estrella's house. Tavera comes out and recognises him. The king tells him that he desires to see his house, but Tavera, though with respect, refuses him admission. Don Arias, the confidant, however manages to get in and telling Estrella of the king's passion offers her on his behalf the wealth of Castile. He offers her towns of which she shall be suzerain and for husband a gentleman of birth. The virtuous creature refuses with scorn. Then he suborns her slave and maidservant. Under a promise in black and white (since the promises of kings are often broken), of freedom and a thousand ducats a year, she agrees to betray her mistress. When Tavera is out and not expected back till dawn she introduces the king into the house. But before he has set eyes on Estrella, Tavera returns and, coming upon a strange man, is about to kill him when the king (not so brave as his name indicates) tells him who he is. Busto Tavera feigns not to believe him. It is impossible that the king, disguised and alone, should have forced his way into his loyal subject's house and he swears to punish the intruder for venturing to make such a pretence. Swords are drawn. The noise brings in servants and in the confusion the king escapes. Tavera guesses that it is the slave who has let the king in and forces her to confess. He upbraids his sister for having thus dishonoured him, but convinced by her protestations that she was no party to what has happened, decides to marry her at once to Don Sancho Ortiz. For himself he will seek safety in flight.

The king, frustrated and angry, decides to have Tavera killed. His confidant suggests a safe man to do the deed. This is no other than Don Sancho Ortiz. While they are talking they see a body swinging from a rope. It is the slave with the king's written promise in her hand. The king sends for Don Sancho and orders him to kill a man who has grossly outraged him. He promises in reward to grant him any boon he asks. He tells him that he may kill the man by guile, but this Don Sancho proudly refuses to do; he will kill him only in fair fight. The king gives him a written order so that he may disculpate himself, but Don Sancho, very imprudently trusting in the king's word, tears it up. Then the king hands him another paper on which is written the victim's name. When Don Sancho leaves the palace the news is brought him that Tavera has decided that he shall marry Estrella immediately. He is transported with delight. But he opens the paper the king has given him and sees with horror that it is Tavera he must kill. He loves him more than a brother; he realises that if he kills him he will lose Estrella; but his hesitation is short; his loyalty to the king

bids him put away his private feelings, and meeting
Tavera he picks a quarrel and kills him. The dying
man leaves Estrella to his protection. The alcaldes
of the city come, accompanied by guards, and arrest
him. While Estrella is dressing for her wedding
the alcaldes bring to the house the body of Busto Tavera
and tell her that it is her lover who has killed him.

(Attaboy, that'll knock 'em. Gee!)

The king is informed that Don Sancho confesses to
the murder, but will not say why he committed it,
whereupon he sends to him with the command that
he shall tell his reasons for the wilful deed and if he has
a paper to prove what he says, produce it. Don Sancho
says that he has no paper (we have indeed seen him
destroy it before the king's eyes) and being sworn to
secrecy can say nothing. Though betrayed, he will not
betray. Then Estrella goes to the king and begs him
to give up Don Sancho to her so that she may herself
avenge her murdered brother. The king, thinking she
will kill him and glad of a way out of his very awkward
predicament, gives her an order to the governor of the
prison. She presents herself disguised and when her
lover is handed over to her, tells him that she has
provided for him a horse and money so that he may
escape. Don Sancho, not recognising her (it was well
known that when you were disguised even your own
mother couldn't know you) desires to know to whom
he owes his liberty and eventually forces her to discover

herself. When he sees Estrella he refuses to accept it and notwithstanding her entreaties returns to his prison. Meanwhile, Don Arias, the confidant, has tried to induce the king to acknowledge that Tavera was murdered by his order; but this the king cannot bring himself to do. He fears the anger of Seville and the effect on Castile of a report of such treachery. The resourceful confidant then suggests that he should persuade the justices to commute the death penalty to banishment. The justices are sent for. The king gives them plausible reasons for the step he desires them to take, but they plead the majesty of the law; they represent the king and, though as vassals he may command them anything, as judges they must act according to their conscience: Don Sancho must die. The king is troubled and confused; he is indeed in a most embarrassing situation. Now Don Sancho and Estrella are introduced. Don Sancho still refuses to speak. He demands death so that he may atone for the killing of his friend. The king is shattered by all this nobility and admits at last that it was he who gave the order for Tavera's despatch. The justices yield; if the king did this it could only be because he had just cause; not theirs to reason why. Don Sancho, exonerated, will go into voluntary exile and reminding the king of his promise to grant him whatever boon he demands asks that Estrella should become his wife. The king, perhaps thinking that she has caused him quite enough trouble, is willing, but Estrella declares that she cannot eat the bread and sleep in the bed of Busto Tavera's assassin.

'Sir,' she tells the king, 'though I love and adore him, the man who killed my brother can never be my spouse.'

'And I,' adds Sancho, somewhat tamely, 'though I love her, see that it would be unjust.'

Thus the play ends. Not the least of its merits is that it has hardly any comic relief. You would have thought that with ballads and dances and comediettas during the intervals the Spanish audience had enough distraction to enable them to support the seriousness of a three-act play. Not so. The comic servant was obligatory. His business was to pair off with the heroine's maid, and in La Hermosa Fea, as though Lope were ridiculing the tedious convention, the Gracioso complains that for once there is no waiting woman for him to marry. But I have a notion that his dramatic purpose was not only to give the groundlings occasion for laughter: with his realistic attitude and caustic sarcasm he represented the opposition of common sense to the idealism and high-flown bombast of the other personages. They might sacrifice themselves for love or duty, they might risk their lives for honour's sake, the Gracioso was there to point out that a wench, a square meal and a whole skin were better than all your heroics. He was so popular a figure because he corresponded with something deep and permanent in the Spanish temper. They have always recognised that there were two sides in them, and that is why (somewhat late in the day, it is true), they have accepted Cervantes' immortal novel as a true epitome of their character. They are at the same time the Knight of the Dolorous Countenance and Sancho Panza. Perhaps they were never more conscious of this than during the Golden Age. They had conquered vast empires in America and all Europe acknowledged their power; but they were hungry, they were hungry all the time. Some force impelled them to foolhardy adventures of universal conquest, and to the even more perilous adventures of the spirit, and they hazarded them because they could not help themselves; but all the time, at the back of their minds, was the uneasy feeling that all this was moonshine, and a full belly and a bed to sleep on were the only realities.

Lope had a lively sense of humour and he made his Graciosos living persons; they were ingenious rascals, ironists with a cynical wit; but with Calderon they are only ignorant clowns. Calderon had no vestige of humour and his comic servants are of a monstrous dullness. Outside Spain Calderon is the most celebrated of the Spanish dramatists. The romantics at the beginning of the nineteenth century held him in high esteem and their judgment has been accepted by succeeding generations who have not much bothered about him, La Vida es Sueño has the reputation of being a great play. I am not sure that it is his best. I think it is more admired than read. Calderon had of course notable merits. He had the mystical feeling, common to many Spaniards of his age, that the world of sense we live in is but a part of the spiritual world and to this owes its significance. It gives certain of his plays a nobility that dramatists have seldom achieved. They say he was a great poet, but speaking with the diffidence proper to a foreigner, I should have said that it was his mind that was poetic; to me his verse is monotonous and the conceits with which, following the fashion of the time, he stuffed it full, are wearisome. He had an intolerable verbosity, and when he sets out on a poetic flight it seems as though nothing could stop him. He had little power of invention. He had no sense of character. Few of his personages live. But he had personality, a grim, cold and yet passionate personality; and personality, I think, is the only thing that keeps a writer alive. With all his faults he can be read now more easily than Lope de Vega. There is in such of his plays as I have read (for I have read but a dozen out of the couple of hundred he wrote) a sense of the mystery of things that can hardly fail to move. You seem to hear in the distance, faintly audible, while this or the other is happening, the sinister drums of unseen powers. But it is not my business to offer the reader a criticism of Calderon. My interest in him is for the light he throws on the character of the Spaniards of his day. His great success proves that his instincts corresponded with the prepossessions of his audience.

His religious sense was profound, and indeed, after having a natural son or two, he was ordained. (The Spanish writers were prolific not only with their pens; they produced enough bastards to man a regiment and fill the nunneries of a fair-sized town.) He was passionately faithful to the Church and only naturally expected the Church to do the right thing by him. When he was not given certain preferment that he expected he wrote to the Cardinal-Archbishop and said he would write no more plays till the injustice was remedied. It was. Happy days for the dramatist! Now, a playwright's decision to write no more would be accepted with equanimity. At the time he wrote the condition of Spain was desperate; ruin faced the country and a large part of its territory was wrested from the Spanish crown. The Spaniards clung all the more fiercely to the faith that had once seemed their greatest glory. But it was a cruel faith, cruel to those that practised its precepts and cruel to those that neglected them. With many it was no more than an extravagant and senseless superstition. In an outrageous play called La Devocion de la Cruz, Calderon allows his hero, guilty of shocking crimes, to be saved because he has always had a devotion to the Cross, and while he committed them had consistently trusted in its efficacy for salvation. And Don Fernando, Prince of Portugal, when captured by the King of Morocco refuses to allow the city of Ceuta to be surrendered to ransom him because the Portuguese had made it Catholic and he could not suffer its churches to be turned into mosques. The thought of it in his own words strikes him mute (which however does not prevent him from going on for another hundred lines), takes his breath away, chokes him with pain, breaks his heart, raises his hair on end and leaves him all of a tremble.

But in this scene there are two fine lines. The audience may very well have thought them sublime.

Por qué ne me das á Ceuta?

Porque es de Dios y no es mia.

'Why,' the king asks his captive, 'will you not give me Ceuta?'

'Because it is God's, not mine.'

Another thing that makes Calderon's plays interesting is his preoccupation with the point of honour, and here again one can imagine that he faithfully portrayed the ruling passion of the times. For honour was an obsession. It is not too much to say that it was as strong a motive for the Spaniard's fidelity to the church as was his fear of hell. Even the picaroons are sensitive of their honour and will stick at nothing to avenge an affront upon it. A slight unknown to any but him who suffers it, a suspicion thrown on the virtue of his wife, though he knows it to be unfounded, will rankle, depriving a man of sleep, driving him crazy, till he can wipe it out in blood. In no play of Calderon's is this more clearly shown than in El Medico de su Honra. Though he loves his wife passionately and knows that she loves him, when Don Gutierre discovers that the king's brother has taken a fancy to her he is distracted with jealousy. Doña Mencia, his wife, has refused to listen to the prince's declarations, but he knows that the prince has set foot in his house. He has no doubt that she is faithful to him, but cannot endure the outrage to his honour. He kills her in cold blood. And in El Alcalde de Zalamea, to my mind Calderon's finest play, the mayor when the captain of a troop on the march to Portugal seizes and rapes his daughter, begs the seducer on his bended knees to marry her. Though a peasant he is rich and he offers the seducer all his fortune if he will make good by marriage the wrong he has done. The captain scornfully refuses to mingle his noble blood with that of a peasant. When the mayor realises that the captain will not make amends, sternly, but with expressions of great respect for his quality, he has him strangled. Only thus can the injury be satisfied.

The life of the actors was, as Cervantes said, one of intolerable labour. They were up at dawn to learn their parts. They rehearsed from nine to twelve, dined and went to the theatre; they left it at seven; and then, however tired, if important people wanted them, the mayor, the judge or what not, off they had to traipse and give a show. They earned their bread in the sweat of their brows; and Agustin de Rojas, of whom I have already spoken, said that there was not a negro in Spain nor a slave in Algiers whose lot was harder than theirs. He has left a lively picture of the life led by these strolling players on the road. Agustin de Rojas was celebrated for the loas he wrote, the monologues with which the performances at the theatre began, and wanting to publish them he hit upon an ingenious device. He contrived a series of conversations between four actors, Rios, Ramirez, Solano and himself, as they wandered from city to city to fulfil their engagements, and to while away the tediousness of the journeys, for they went on foot, he recited to them his loas. His companions must have been good natured to listen to some of them. Their ingenuity is very trying. They bristle with conceits and abound in learning, biblical, mythological and historical. Some praise the merits of the cities the actors are about to visit; there is one in praise of the letter A and another in praise of the days of the week. The amusing ones are those in which the author vivaciously narrates his own adventures. Perhaps the reader will not have forgotten the curious love story that emerges from his tale. Fortunately he needed a good deal of padding, and between his recitations the four players talk of one thing and another. On one occasion Rios recounts his experiences on a certain journey as follows.

'We left the city of Valencia, Solano and I, on account

of a misfortune, one of us on foot and without a cloak, and the other walking and with only a doublet. We gave our traps to a boy who got lost in the town and so we were left gentlemen of the road. We arrived at a village at night, exhausted, with only eight cuartos between us. Having nothing to eat we went to a hostelry and asked for a bed, but they said there was none to be had because there was a fair. Seeing the small chance there was of our finding one, I went to an inn and said that I was a merchant from the Indies. The hostess asked me if we had pack-horses and I answered that we had come by cart and that while our goods were coming she should make us up a couple of beds and prepare supper. She did so, and I went to the mayor of the village and telling him that a company of players was passing through asked his leave to act a play. He asked me if it was religious. I told him it was and he gave me leave; I went back to the inn and told Solano to run over the auto of Cain and Abel and then go to a certain place and collect money because we were to give a show that night. Meanwhile I went to look for a drum, made a beard out of a piece of sheepskin and went through the whole village announcing my play. There were a lot of people in the place and many came. This done, I put the drum aside, took off my beard and going to the hostess told her that my goods were arriving and she must give me a key to the door of my room so that I could lock them up. She asked me what they were and I said grocery.

She gave me the key and I took the sheets off the bed
and pulled down an old hanging and two or three bits
of stuff and so that I shouldn't be seen coming down,
made them into a bundle, threw it out of the window and
flew down like the wind. When I got to the yard the
host called me and said: Master Indian, d'you want to
see a show by some strolling players who have just
come? It's good. I said I'd go and hurriedly went to
look for the things that we were to act our play with, but
though I looked everywhere I couldn't find them. Faced
with this blow as the job might get me a whipping, I ran
to where Solano was taking in the money, told him what
had happened and said that he must stop collecting and
we'd better make ourselves scarce with the cash. . . .
That night we didn't go far and we kept off the high
road, and in the morning we counted our money. We
found three and a half reals in small change. Picture us
wandering on, with money, but a bit scared; after about
a league we saw a hovel, and when we reached it they
treated us to wine from a gourd, milk from a trough and
bread from saddle-bags. We had breakfast and that
night got to another village where we set about earning
our supper. I asked for leave to give a performance, got
a couple of sheets, advertised the show, got a guitar,
invited the woman of the inn and told Solano to collect
the money. Finally, before a full house, I came out and
sang the ballad, 'Afuera, afuera; aparta, aparta'; after one
couplet I dried up and the public couldn't make it out,

but Solano began a loa and so made up for the shortage
of music. I dressed myself in a sheet and began my part,
and when Solano appeared as God the Father, with the
other sheet on, but open in the middle, his beard stained
with grape-skins and a candle in his hand, I thought I
should die of laughing. The wretched public didn't
know what had happened to him. After this I came on
as a clown and did my entremes, then went on with the
play; but when I came to the point of killing the
miserable Abel I'd forgotten the knife to cut his throat,
so I took off my beard and cut it with that. It caused an
uproar and the crowd began to yell. I begged them to
forgive our shortcomings as the company hadn't arrived
yet. At last the audience struck and the inn-keeper came
and told us to get out because they wanted to give us a
hiding. On this grand advice we made tracks and went
off that very night with no more than the five reals we'd
made. After spending this, selling the little we had left,
often eating the mushrooms that we picked by the way,
sleeping on the ground, walking barefoot (not on
account of the mud, but because we had no shoes),
helping the muleteers to load up, watering mules,
and living for more than four days on turnips, we slunk
in to an inn one night where four carters who were there
gave us twenty maravedis and a blood-pudding to give
them a show. Leading this wretched existence, with all
these misfortunes, we reached the end of our journey,
Solano in his doublet, without his coat (which he'd

pawned at an inn), and I bare-legged and shirtless, with a great straw hat full of holes, dirty linen breeches and my coat all torn and threadbare. I was in such rags I made up my mind to take a job with a pastry-cook, but Solano was so grand he wouldn't work. And then all of a sudden, when we were in this mess we heard the beating of a drum and a boy advertising a show: the good play, Los Amigos Trocados, is being presented to-night at the town-hall. When I heard this my eyes opened as wide as a calf's. We spoke to the boy and when he recognised us he dropped his drum and began to dance for joy. I asked him if he had any money hidden away and he took out what he had wrapped in the tail of his shirt. We bought bread, cheese and a cut of dried cod (which was very good there) and after eating went to find the manager (who was Martinazos), but I don't know whether he was glad to see us when he saw how beggarly we were. Anyhow he greeted us and after we'd given him an account of all our trials, we had dinner and then he told us to delouse ourselves, because he was going to let us act and he didn't want a lot of lice in the costumes. That night, in fact, we helped him and next day he gave us a contract for three-quarters of a real per show . . . We led this cheerful life for rather more than four weeks, eating little, travelling a lot, with our properties on our backs, and never saw a bed the whole blessed time.'

I do not imagine that anyone can read this story

without thinking it lucky for Rios that he had high spirits. He must have been a man whom it was difficult to disconcert. He was certainly no fool. When one of the party lamented the fickleness of some young person who had left him when he had no more money, he delivered himself of the following remarks:

'Brother,' he said, 'women are like bird-lime; good at sticking and bad at letting go. When a man spends his money on them and gives them presents, they do the dirty on him. And if he gives them nothing they say he's as mean as cat's meat. If he lets them gad about as much as they like, they think he's a fool; and if he won't, they think he's a bore. If he's in love with them they can't bear the sight of him and if he isn't, they won't give him a moment's peace.'

'A girl, a vineyard, a pear-tree and a beanfield want a deal of looking after,' observed one of the others.

'Sir,' he replied, 'you can't have a woman without a fault or a mule without a sire.'

IX

THOUGH the sun might never set on the Spanish King's dominions and his fleets brought from the Indies year after year precious metals that to the imagination of the time appeared of fantastic value, his chosen people suffered from hunger. To get not enough to eat, but enough to prevent them from dying of starvation, was their constant preoccupation. Half the dull rogueries that the picaroons committed were to get food to put in their bellies. The monasteries daily provided all comers with a dish of soup and to get this thieves and students, beggars, soldiers and artisans waited patiently at their gates. The famished scholar and the starveling gentleman were stock figures of fun. When a gallant wanted to show his appreciation of his lady's charm he sent her food, not chocolates like the lover of to-day, but sausages and a ham, a pasty and a brace of capons. Far from offending her delicacy such a present was accepted with eagerness.

But this did not impair their cheerfulness. They were perfectly ready to make a joke of an empty belly and they could have a good time on dry bread, an onion and a drink of water: a gay and laughter-loving people, passionately addicted to amusement. I have told already how fond they were of the theatre. Beside this they had bull-fights, public shows and religious processions. A festival of the church was a public holiday. Then the house-fronts were decorated with bright hangings, women, young and old, thronged the balconies and the chattering, vivacious crowd surged in the streets. They never tired of going on little excursions to the Prado in Madrid or to the Alameda de Hércules in Seville. Men of quality went on horseback and the women, in all their bravery, their faces white with powder and their cheeks vermilion with cinnabar, on foot or by carriage. Then if no gallant accompanied them they were ready enough to enter upon a flirtatious contest of wits with a stranger. They did not hesitate to ask him to buy them oranges, sweets and other kickshaws from the wandering vendors. At sunset they ate the supper they had brought with them. All classes frequented these cool and pleasant places; the artisan with his wife and children picnicked happily in the immediate neighbourhood of the fine lady with her duenna and attendant swains. They relished back-chat and a gift for repartee made a man famous. Wherever people assembled, they amused themselves with the thrust and parry of persiflage. A woman was admired if she had a sharp reply to a wanton jest and you were sure of the applause of the crowd if you managed to make an inoffensive stranger look a fool.

It was the same spirit that made them take so much delight in practical jokes. This lamentable form of humour was of course practised at that time throughout Europe, but I think it was nowhere more prevalent than in Spain. The soil was favourable. The jokes played were coarse and brutal. Their aim was to subject the victim to an intolerable humiliation and since the Spaniard's honour meant so much to him he was more than others susceptible to the shame that was put upon him. People who read Don Quixote are outraged at the cruel game that is made of the gentle, crazy knight and indeed but for the enchanting conversations between master and man it would be hard to read the book now without distress. But to the readers of Cervantes' day these pranks were matter for uproarious mirth. They are at all events less foul than many you find in the masterpieces of picaresque literature. In Quevedo's El Buscon (a repository of practical jokes) an incident is related that is significant of the manners of the day. When the hero (a proper rascal certainly) went to study at Alcalá de Henares and, as was not unusual, to keep himself, acted as servant to a richer undergraduate, on going for the first time to the university he was surrounded by the students who with jeers and mocking laughter spat on him from head to foot till face and clothes were white as snow with spittle. In all the books I have read I do not remember more than one such jest that has brought a smile to my lips. For its rarity I will narrate it.

A serving-man, waiting for his master at the city gate of Guadalajara, saw a funeral procession approach. Half a dozen priests, solemnly chanting, four friars and a number of mourners. He called to them with a loud voice to stop. More surprised by the novelty of the occasion than impressed by his appearance they did so, and one of the priests asked him what he wanted.

'Who is the deceased?' he asked.

'If it matters to you could you not have asked while we were going rather than stop us?'

He insisted that it was important for them to stay and tell him what he wished to know. They answered him:

'The deceased is a weaver called Juan de Paracuellos. He died in four days from kidney trouble. He leaves a wife, young and poor, called Maria de la O, and three children of whom the eldest is not six. Now of what importance is it that you should have this tiresome information?'

One of the dead man's two brothers who were following the bier told them to go on.

'Stop, I repeat,' cried the joker. 'And you, defunct weaver, by the power and virtue of my charmed words, I order you to rise hale and hearty and return to the tangled making of your stuffs.'

They all marvelled to hear this mysterious exorcism

and put the bier down on the ground. Attracted by the noise the neighbours, men, women and children, crowded round.

'For the second time,' he went on, 'I command you, obstinate corpse, to rise hale and hearty and return to finish the cloth that you had begun.'

None of those present could make up his mind whether this was a madman or a wizard who in the sight of all dared to make so strange a charge. Neither his face nor his habit suggested the saint. They paused. They stared, without so much as batting an eyelash, at the dead man, and the joker raising his voice still more cried out once again:

'For the third and last time of asking, I order you, dead weaver, to rise good and proper and return to wield the shuttle which is the means of livelihood of your family.'

The disobedient corpse did not stir; whereupon the rogue said:

'Pass on, gentlemen, and proceed with the funeral, for I give you my word that the same thing has happened to me twice with two dead men at Toledo and Ocana, and neither of them would be resuscitated. And pardon me for having detained you.'

Having said this he took to his heels followed by the enraged populace. He took refuge in a monastery and having told the monks what had happened they were so much amused that they helped him to get safely away.

This story is told by Tirso de Molina in a tedious book called Las Cigarrales de Toledo.

But for all this brutality the Spaniards in their mutual intercourse preserved the forms of scrupulous politeness. Ceremonial phrases were part and parcel of ordinary conversation. It was no more than civil to say 'I kiss your mercy's hands,' or 'I put myself at your mercy's feet.' The Habsburg dynasty had brought with it a passion for titles and their possessors addressed one another by them with great punctiliousness. Common and gentle alike set great store on purity of descent and well they might since a trace of Jewish or Moorish blood brought with it all manner of disabilities. They were enraptured with their own nobility and both men and women seldom told you the story of their lives (an inveterate habit of theirs) without stating from what eminent families they issued. In one play, Lope's El Premio del Bien Hablar, the heroine, knowing that her suitor wants something to read, sends him her family tree to show him that her extraction is no less aristocratic than his. Lope, whose father was an embroiderer, claimed descent from a noble family of Asturias, and even the wise Cervantes, the son of a surgeon-barber who wandered from town to town cupping and blistering his patients, laid claim without justification to the distinguished name of Saavedra. In passing I may mention an incident that I came across in a life of Solorzano, a voluminous writer of picaresque stories. He was for some time secretary to the Conde de Benavente, a famous Viceroy of Naples, and the king desiring to reward his services at no expense to himself granted him a title with the right to sell it. He disposed of it, doubtless at a good price, to a certain Vicencio Antoniani, a native of Gaeta. It has occurred to me that this is a practice that might very well be followed at the present day: the needy servant of the state might thus be spared financial anxiety in his old age at no cost to the tax-payer and many a prosperous merchant or lucky broker might honourably join the ranks of the aristocracy.

Van Aarssens, the Dutch traveller, says that the streets of Madrid were large, but foul and stinking. 'They which calculate all the ordures cast into them say they are daily perfumed by above a hundred thousand close-stools.' Everyone threw his slops out of window, though if he were law-abiding only from ten at night till day-break, and this custom also gave occasion for practical jokes that were much appreciated. This inconvenience, however, would hardly have struck the young man whose adventures in Spain were occupying my fancy, for whether he came from Edinburgh or London he would have been familiar with it. The streets were lit at night only by the lamps that burned before the various images. They were far from safe. You ran the danger of being set upon by a band of ruffians who might leave you dead and stripped of everything that you had on you. If a gentleman had a grudge against another he did not hesitate to have him waylaid by hired assassins and stabbed to death. For the point of honour did not make the unreasonable demand that you should risk your own skin to dispose of an enemy when you could pay others to do the job for you. Nor did the path of courtship run without hazard. Women in theory lived in a seclusion almost as great as in Moorish times, the windows on the street were few and protected by the reja, the grille, typical of Spain, on which the ironworkers of the period lavished such charming invention; and from behind them they exchanged at night pleasant conceits with their admirers. But the gallant was so jealous, and so arrogant, that often he would not even suffer another in the same street and swords were drawn to decide which should remain. Sometimes a stern parent or a punctilious brother would issue from the house and at the rapier's point drive away the unwelcome suitor.

I have already mentioned the fact that love was an affection that seized upon its victims at first sight. In men and women equally (at least in plays and novels) a glance, a comely shape seen in passing, could excite a paroxysm of passion. So ardent was it that even early in the morning, and the dawn was the signal for them to rise, its power engrossed them. I think I am not wrong in saying that in our day, on the other hand, the passion misnamed tender has a very small hold on the lover till the first cocktail has brought its solace and its violence can be held within the bounds of common sense till after business hours. In Spain they loved twenty-four hours a day. They were a race who spoke naturally in an exaggerated fashion, and when we would say, 'What a bore,' they would cry, 'Is there in the whole world a more unhappy man than I?' I have already related in what terms the rude soldier Miguel de Castro referred to his beloved. The Spanish lover snatched down the moon from heaven to lay at his lady's feet; the sun was dragged in by his flaming hair; he ransacked classical mythology to prove the extravagance of his desire and the animal and vegetable kingdoms only just sufficed to provide him with metaphors. It was a love the aim of which was marriage, especially when the lady's birth and fortune were of a satisfactory nature, but whether this was due to the censorship of the Inquisition or the Spaniard's innate desire for domesticity I do not know.

But the love that enflamed these hot-blooded people, notwithstanding their romantic professions, was very honestly, without pretences on one side or the other, rooted in sexual desire. Marriage was but the necessary prelude to the nuptial couch. But men being what they were and women healthily eager to share their pleasure, the marriage ceremony was often anticipated and then it was difficult to induce the gallant to fulfil his promises. On the Spanish stage there is a long procession of high-born ladies mourning their lost honour and through three acts pursuing the faithless lover with entreaties or threats of vengeance. The stage rings with their appeals for justice. They do not attempt to conceal their shame, but lament it vociferously in every kind of metrical form. It must be admitted that when the unwilling swain is obliged, willy-nilly, to redeem his pledge he does so with a good grace and the spectator is left with the consoling assurance that the couple will live happily ever after.

Considering their obstinate persuasion that in their virginity they possess a pearl of great price, the female characters of the Spanish drama are astonishingly careless about it. The dangers that attend its loss are constantly before their eyes. Not only may the ravisher leave them in the lurch, but their fathers and brothers may think that only their death can cleanse the blot on their escutcheon. In El Alcalde de Zalamea, when Isabel has been abducted by soldiers and ravished by their captain, her brother, though but a peasant's son, is only prevented from plunging his dagger in her heart by the opportune appearance of their father. She, poor thing, though in no way to blame, looks upon death as no more than her due. When she finds her father tied to a tree she will not unloose him, convinced that he will kill her before she has said her say, till in melodious numbers she has given him a circumstantial account of the outrage that has been inflicted on her. Her father however decides that it will do if she enters a convent. As the bride of Jesus Christ, he remarks with brutal common sense, she chooses a husband who is not fussy over quality. But notwithstanding these hazards the feckless creatures continue to exhibit an extreme want of prudence. They are more negligent of that article of virtue, their maidenhead, than ever an actress of our day of a heavily insured string of pearls.

In this connection it is instructive to examine a play called El Burlador de Sevilla which has made some stir in the world. It is by Gabriel Tellez, a Mercenarian monk who wrote under the name of Tirso de Molina; and I may remark in passing that he managed the affairs of his order and performed his religious duties in an exemplary manner. It must be one of the worst plays that was ever written. The Spanish dramatists, perhaps rightly, never bothered themselves much with rules, but few plays can ever have run their course in so happy-go-lucky a fashion as does this one. It is monstrously incoherent. Scenes follow one another with no sequence. Probability is flouted. Peasants indulge in conceits that would have surprised even the cultured Euphues. None of the persons behaves with elementary common sense. The characters are perfectly conventional. Nowadays when a play is badly constructed, when its people act without rhyme or reason, and loose ends are left lying about all over the place, we sit up and say it has atmosphere. I suppose one might say of El Burlador de

Sevilla that it had the same vague quality. It has certainly a strange, sinister life. One cannot, however, read it without being astonished that such a clumsy piece of work should have had such a remarkable destiny. Innumerable versions have been made of it. It has inspired poets and painters, sculptors and composers. For it is in this play that Don Juan first made his bow before a world that has never since been tired of gazing at him. It proves, I suppose, that you may write as badly as you like, and do your job as ill as it can be done, if you chance to create a type he will go marching down the ages to the end of time. You gave him life and he holds you for ever in the remembrance of men. It is the best fortune that can ever happen to an author.

Don Quixote, Sancho Panza and Don Juan Tenorio are all three immortal.

It is curious to compare the Don Juan of this play with the Don Juan that posterity has little by little constructed. But first of all let it be noted that the episode of the statue coming to supper has been a great stumbling-block. Authors in fact have found him (or it) the very devil to deal with. After his entrance, which cannot fail to be dramatic, they have none of them quite known what to do with him. Tirso de Molina made a greater hash of it than any of his successors. The statue comes to supper with Don Juan and then Don Juan goes to supper with him. By making two scenes when only one was necessary the dramatist has lamentably

weakened his effect. But it was this incident that gave
him the idea for his play and through its course he was
bound to work up to it. He invented the character of
Don Juan to fit it. Tirso de Molina is not the only playwright whose imagination has been excited by a dramatic
incident and when he came to write his play found that
the character he had devised to act it made the incident
nonsensical. Don Juan lives in despite of the paltry
intrigue and the grotesque catastrophe. Later generations have represented him as a great lover, passionate
but inconstant, and it was inevitable that some should
have seen in his unsatisfied desire an allegory of life.
Others have looked upon his fickleness as a symbol of
man's restless seeking for the ideal. Some have thought
that he passed from one earthly love to another in desperate pursuit of that heavenly love of which Plato
wrote. But Tirso called his play El Burlador de Sevilla,
The Joker of Seville. His Don Juan is not a great lover,
he is a great fornicator. But his pleasure lies not only in
the gratification of his lust, but in the joke of it; half the
fun consists in the deceit he has practised. He gets
women by stratagem, by promises he has no intention
of fulfilling, by making much of his position, and when
he has had his way with them is tickled to death because
he has made fools of them. It is a jest of the same nature
as pulling away a chair when somebody is just going to
sit on it. Prudence and courage are strangely mingled in
him. He will hazard his life to save his servant from

drowning, but he prepares his get-away at the same time as he makes arrangements to seduce his victim. He can afford to be bold since he takes no risks; his father is chief justice and the king's favourite. He is a good Catholic, and though he turns a sarcastic ear to such as threaten him with the vengeance of heaven, he fully intends to make his peace with God in good time. He is incapable of gratitude and insensitive to others' pain. He is gallant, witty and courteous. The type lives on; Don Juan is the ancestor of the raffish young nobleman of our own day, with the manners of a gentleman and the instincts of a Borstal boy, who makes his friends of prize-fighters, jockeys and bar-loungers. Good-natured and unscrupulous, he is described by the people who like him as his own worst enemy. A frightful bounder. Women, though he treats them like kitchen-maids, adore him. They fall for him with such indecent alacrity that he himself is often embarrassed. Strange creatures! Gangsters and crooks will tell you that what makes their trade so hard is neither the vigilance of the police nor the untrustworthiness of their confederates but the importunity of the sex.

And indeed the behaviour of the women in El Burlador de Sevilla is so imprudent, their folly so inane, that it almost serves to disculpate the ruffian. The Duchess Isabella, a maiden, admits into her room at night a man who knocks at the door and hops into bed with her under the impression that it is her suitor. She is very much surprised when a light is brought to discover that she has lost her virginity to a total stranger. Tisbea is a fisher-girl, and when Don Juan has just escaped drowning she gives him shelter in her hut. He has but to promise her marriage for her immediately to succumb to his advances. Doña Ana loves and is beloved of the Marques de la Mota, Don Juan's dearest friend. She has made an appointment with him, whereupon Don Juan, getting rid of him by a trick, takes his place and ravishes her. Aminta, a pretty peasant, is being married to Batricio when Don Juan casts his eye on her. He tells Batricio that he has already slept with her, whereupon the bridegroom's honour forces him to leave her. Don Juan makes his way into the wedding-chamber and after telling her what a grand fellow he is (and of course promising marriage) seduces her. It may be that the maidenhead of these women, duchess or peasant, is their most priceless possession; they are all in a confounded hurry to be rid of it. Not thus behaved the heroine of the novel La Picara Justina. She knew very well the worth of her virtue and with wiles and her quick wit foiled the attempts of the men, students, barbers, pious hermits and sanctimonious sacristans, who sought to debauch her; she plundered them all and gave nothing in return, so that when at last she married she was able to say with pride that her virginity would honourably prove itself by enamelling with ruby floods the silvery

174

white of the nuptial sheets. Messy, but convincing!

But there are people so perverse as to declare that novels and plays do not always give a trustworthy picture of the manners and customs of the day. They point to our London stage, with its murders and burglaries, its crooks and gangsters, and claim that an intelligent foreigner making a tour of it would get a very false impression of the average life of the English. I will quote then, in this connection, from A Journey into Spain by the eminently respectable van Aarssens, Heer van Sommerledijk. 'Besides the great numbers of loose women that are to be found up and down Madrid,' he writes, 'there are others in certain fixed quarters, countenanced by Publick Authority, for accommodation of any that will go to them. . . . They have a salary from the Town, for which cause so infamous an employment is sought after, and when one of the Jades dies or is disabled by the Pox, the Magistrates are sollicited for the vacancy. . . . Sinning thus with impunity and toleration of Publick Authority, they seldom forsake the vice they so openly profess, though one day in the year is devoted to exhort them to repentance: On a Friday in Lent, they are by an alguazil or two conducted to the Church of Penitents, and there seated near the Pulpit, where the Preacher does his best to touch their hearts, but seldom with success; after many vain exhortations to amend their lives, descending from his Pulpit, he presents them the Crucifix, saying

Behold the Lord, embrace him; which if any does, she is immediately taken away, and shut up in the Cloister of Penitents; but usually they only hang down their heads and shed a few tears, without laying hold on what is offered, and after their grimaces continue their deboshed life; neither can the story of St. Mary Magdalene so often inculcated to them, move them to imitation of her.'

There is no reason to suppose that the family of the divine Cervantes was very different from any other family in the middle class to which he belonged. There is much in its recorded behaviour that must give pain to the moral sense of our enlightened age. His Aunt Maria became the mistress of an archdeacon, and her father, a stern and upright judge, did not hesitate to invoke the majesty of the law when the reverend gentleman fought shy of paying the stipulated sum to compensate her for the loss of her virtue. The author had two sisters, Magdalena and Andrea, and both supplemented their meagre earnings as sempstresses by the pleasant and more lucrative exercise of prostitution. He would have been released from captivity in Algiers much sooner than he was if Don Alfonso Pacheco de Portocarrera, notwithstanding his illustrious name, had not bilked Magdalena of five hundred ducats. Don Alfonso seems to have been a bad payer. He agreed to pay Andrea five hundred ducats ('for the great obligation to you that I am under'), but the most assiduous research has failed to show that he did so. It looks as though the whole family were like that, for Andrea was obliged to bring an action against his brother for money and jewels that he had promised her. Fortunately for all parties she had other admirers who were more generous. An Italian, Juan Francisco Locadelo, had on one occasion given her a certain sum in cash, wearing apparel and a lot of household furniture. Part of this, five rolls of taffeta, when money was short Cervantes afterwards pawned for thirty ducats.

Shortly before his marriage to Catalina de Salazar, Cervantes had a daughter by an actress called Ana Franca. She was known as Isabel de Saavedra. Her mother dying when she was fourteen or fifteen, her Aunt Magdalena engaged her as a maid-servant. She does not appear to have remained a maid very long and so naturally ceased to be a servant; she then assumed her rightful station as a daughter of the house. This was only proper since, her aunts being long past their prime, it seems to have devolved on her (with Cervantes earning so little by his pen) to keep the home fires burning. For soon after the triumphant publication of Don Quixote a very unfortunate accident befell its author. A rake named Gaspar de Espileta was mortally wounded at the door of his house. He was brought in to die. The Alcalde who undertook the investigation learned that the behaviour of the ladies of the house had given rise to scandal and, thinking that they knew

more of the murder than they chose to say, arrested
Cervantes, his sister Andrea and her bastard daughter
Constanza, his own daughter Isabel and certain
other women who lived there. He arrested also
a wealthy Portuguese, Simon Mendez by name, who
was commonly supposed to be Isabel's lover. There
was no evidence to show that any of them were con-
nected with the crime, but the four alcaldes sitting in
judgement forbade Simon Mendez to have any further
communication with Isabel de Saavedra, and the
women, though released from gaol, were placed under
arrest in their house. Some time afterwards Isabel de
Saavedra was living by herself (dans ses meubles)
under the protection of a married man of mature age
called Juan de Urbina, and it was he who paid her
dowry when (with a baby of eight months old) she
settled down to married life with a certain Luis de
Molina.

Such were the domestic relations of a very distinguished man of letters in the Golden Age of Spanish
literature.

All this has caused the biographers of Cervantes much
uneasiness and they have exercised a great deal of
ingenuity to conceal the fact that he was poor and saw
no disgrace in profiting, when occasion called, by the
frailty of his sisters first and then of his daughter. It is
unreasonable to judge a man of one age by the standards
of another. A popular author nowadays would think it

discreditable to live on the prostitution of his female relations (he would not need to) but he would not hesitate to praise a critic's book in order to get a favourable criticism of his own. Morally there is nothing to choose between one action and the other. Perhaps no one that we know of was more tolerant than Cervantes; but tolerance is not an umbrella that you take when you think it will rain and leave at home when it looks fine; tolerance is a staff that you carry with you always as a support in all the circumstances of life. There is no reason why Cervantes should not have looked upon his own conduct with the same indulgence as upon other people's. We may do the same. From the behaviour of most people you would judge that tolerance is called for only in matters that you care nothing about: on the contrary it is called for in matters about which you care a great deal. It is not the least of the victories that man may win over his ruthless egoism. The biographers of Cervantes have tried to make a saint of him. Folly! An artist needs no whitewashing. You must take him as he is and it is impertinent to deny his failings: without them he would not be the man, and so the artist, that he is. A writer constructs characters by observation, but he only gives them life if they are himself. The more persons he is the more characters he creates. Cervantes was not only the noble Don Quixote, he was the astute and faithful Sancho, the rascally Ginés de Pasamonte, the barber, the Curate, the joking Sansón Carrasco as well. The artist, like the mystic who tries to attain God, is detached in spirit from the world. He has by his nature the freedom which the mystic seeks in the repression of desires. He stands aloof. The artist's right and wrong are not the right and wrong of plain men. Plain men may condemn him if they choose; he shrugs his shoulders and gravely goes his own way. But the plain man were wise to hesitate. There is a great deal of hypocrisy in our judgement of others. We make an ideal picture of ourselves and measure our fellows by it. But when we read the Diary of Pepys or the Confessions of Rousseau, in which a little of the truth is told, when we study the life of Wagner, we are horrified: we forget; we will not look at our private selves. I do not believe that there is any man, who if the whole truth were known of him, would not seem a monster of depravity; and also I believe that there are very few who have not at the same time virtue, goodness and beauty. Cervantes did not hesitate to profit by the looseness of his sisters. He got into so much trouble in the business affairs in which he was from time to time engaged that it is hard to be quite certain of his honesty. He was courageous. He was long suffering. He was gallant. He was magnanimous.

This is a digression. I apologise for it.

I do not know whether 'in this antick of remarques which I have daubed with so many colours,' to quote

again my good Dutchman, the reader will have been as
much surprised as I have been at the picture of the
Spaniards of the Golden Age that presents itself. For my
part I must admit that it does not in the least fit in with
my preconceptions. These are not the dignified, taciturn
and punctilious creatures that most of us imagine
those hidalgos to have been. So great is the difference
between them and the gay, loose and sportive folk who
display themselves in the literature of the day that one
can hardly believe one's eyes. Certainly when one looks
at the long series of El Greco's portraits in the Prado
it is hard to believe that his sitters were the same
people as those who took their part in Tirso de Molina's
Cigarrales de Toledo from which I took the little story
of the practical joker and the dead weaver. One
cannot see those wan and melancholy gentlemen
dressing up in fantastic garb and playing the fool. Van
Aarssens, who went to Spain when Philip IV was king,
says that in public Spaniards seemed very grave,
serious and reserved, 'but in private, and to those
that are familiarly acquainted with them, they act
in a manner so different, you would not take them
for the same persons.' That is interesting. It looks
as though it were a mask they assumed. Why should
they have done so? The House of Austria looked
upon gravity as an essential part of majesty, and the
same traveller tells us that one day the queen, laughing
at dinner at the quips and antics of a buffoon, was

put in mind that to do so ill became a queen of Spain.
The king, as we know, was trained to show his feelings
neither by his manner nor by his expression. His lips
and tongue moved when he spoke, but no gesture
was permitted him and his countenance suffered
no change. It is possible that this impressive solemnity
was imitated by such as were in contact with the
court and so grew to be a mark of gentility. Then,
in Italy and the Low Countries the Spanish lived
among a hostile population quicker-witted than
themselves: stupid people in authority very naturally assume a dignified manner as a defence against
a cleverness they do not understand. It may have
been very useful to them in their relations with these
subject races. But even in their own country they
have always been suspicious of foreigners. They
have kept them at a distance by haughtiness and
ceremony. It is natural enough that these characteristics
should have impressed foreigners, and when writers
came to portray the Spanish in plays and novels it
was only to be expected that they should seize upon
them as typical. And a type once determined dies
hard. Who on the English stage to-day would believe
in a Frenchman who did not gesticulate or a mathematician who was not absent-minded? The Spaniard
whom the writers, starting with Corneille, depicted,
unsmiling, proud, jealous and passionate, obsessed
with his honour, had an obvious dramatic value;

and it is not strange that the authors of the romantic era should have accepted him without demur, for he precisely fitted their demand for the melodramatic picturesque.

But these are merely guesses and the reader can take them or leave them.

X

ONE of the things that attracted me to the subject I had chosen was the possibility of writing about El Greco. He was fond, as we know, of painting good-looking young men and I intended to have my hero sit to him. This would give me an opportunity, I thought, of drawing a portrait of that strange man as I saw him.

Painters, not unnaturally, since so much nonsense has been written on the subject, have always resented writers expressing their opinions on pictures. They have insisted, often with great vehemence, that only the painter can speak of painting with authority, and that the man of letters, looking at a picture from his literary point of view, can know nothing of its specific value. His part is to admire in silence and if he has the money, buy. This seems to me a narrow way of thinking. Doubtless they are right when they claim that only painters should discuss technique, but technique is not the whole of painting. You might as well say that only a dramatist can appreciate a play. The drama also has its technique, though it is not so abstruse as some of its professors like to pretend, but it is the business only of the dramatist. To understand the technique of an art may be a diversion, it may even give the layman the feeling, agreeable to some people, of being in the know (like addressing the head-waiter of a fashionable restaurant by his first name), but it is not essential to appreciation. It may greatly interfere with it. We know that painters are often very bad judges of pictures, for their interest in technique absorbs them so that they cannot recognise merits, unconnected with it, that may give a picture value. For technique is only the method by which the artist achieves his aim. It is no more than the knowledge that has gradually been acquired of the best ways to attain the specific excellencies of which a medium is capable. It cannot touch the heart nor excite the mind. An inadequate technique will not prevent the artist from doing this. I do not think people are sufficiently conscious of the great difference there is between the attitude of the artist towards the work he creates and the attitude of the beholder. The connection between them is slight. For the moment I will leave on one side the position of the artist and consider the work of art in relation with the beholder.

But first I should like to deal with the meaning of a word. To the term artist is now attached a judgement of value, and (though painters are not so squeamish) most of us who practise an art are as shy of calling ourselves artists as we are of calling ourselves gentlemen. In this sense the term is the sport of fashion. A painter may be at one period considered an artist and at another a charlatan. What makes it more confusing is that it does not always correspond with preëminence. I suppose few people would deny that Addison was a greater artist than Charles Dickens, but few could doubt which was the greater writer. The word craftsman has unfortunate associations, nor does it indicate the act of creation, which is the essence of the matter; and the word creator is intolerably pretentious. I do not know any word that will do but artist; I must use it, but I mean by it only someone who is engaged in the arts. He may be a good artist or a bad one.

I have long since abjured the heresy prevalent in my youth of art for art's sake. Oscar Wilde popularized it in England and Oscar Wilde learnt it from Whistler. It gave art an esoteric quality that flattered the artist and it was accepted by the cultured public with the humility that characterises them. The cultured public have always taken a masochistic pleasure in the contempt that artists have shown them and, browbeaten and intimidated, have comforted themselves with a feeling of superiority over the common herd. It was believed that the object of a work of art was to arouse the æsthetic emotion and when you had felt that you had got all it had to give you. But what is an emotion that results in nothing? To experience the æsthetic emotion is pleasurable and all pleasure is good; but it is pleasurable also to drink a glass of beer and no one has ever been able to show that, taken simply as pleasure, one surpasses the other. Attempts have been made by moralists to prove that spiritual pleasures are keener and more lasting than sensual pleasures; they carry no conviction. No pleasure endures and to please it must be taken in small doses and at not too frequent intervals. It would be no less tedious to hear Beethoven's Fifth Symphony every day than it would be to eat caviare. And until age has blunted the sensibilities the general experience is surely that the pleasures of sense are more vivid than the pleasures of the spirit. We have all known omnivorous readers who read for the delight of it; they absorb books as the machines in Chicago absorb hogs, but no sausages come out of them at the other end; and we have all known the people who moon their days away in picture galleries in imbecile contemplation; they are no better than opium smokers, worse if anything, for the opium smoker at all events is not self-complacent. The value of emotion lies in its effects. Santa Teresa insisted on this over and over again: the ecstasy of union with the Godhead was precious only if it resulted in greater capacity for works. The æsthetic emotion, however delightful and however subtle, has worth only if it leads to action.

The work of art, whether the artist intended it or not, and for my part I think he seldom does, proffers a communication. This has nothing to do with the artist. From his standpoint it may only be a by-product of his activity: so the esculent swallows build nests to rear their young and are unaware that for their aphrodisiac qualities they will go to make soup for the enfeebled but amative Chinese. This communication is made in two voices. For the work of art is a diversion, an escape from the bitterness of life and a solace in the world's inevitable cruelty, a rest from its turmoil and a relief from labour. This is much, and if a work of art has only this communication to make it justifies itself. But great works speak with another voice too; they enrich the soul so that it is capable of a nobler and more fruitful activity. Their effects are worthy deeds. But should you ask me what these are I must confess that I should find it hard to reply. Provisionally at all events I should be willing enough to accept the maxim of Fray Luis de Leon: 'the beauty of life,' he says, 'is nothing but this, that each should act in conformity with his nature and his business.'

Notwithstanding this long preamble I do not wish to say much of El Greco's pictures. Nothing is so tedious as a description of the greens, yellows and blues that are in a picture; you cannot visualise them even with a photograph before you and the narrator's enthusiasm does not matter to you a row of pins. It is enough to say that El Greco's cool, silvery colours are lovely. When the art critics begin to talk of upper triangles and lower triangles, as they do with the Burial of Count Orgaz, or of inner and outer ellipses in the San Maurizio, I sigh. Do they really think that an artist bothers his head with such things? You look at a picture as a whole, that is one of the advantages the plastic arts have over the descriptive, and it is as a whole that it must affect you. The study of its parts is merely amusement. An emotion analysed is no longer an emotion. I do not suppose the painter creates a work of art differently from any other artist. The artist works by instinct combined with knowledge and his knowledge he acquires partly from his predecessors and partly from his own errors. I have had the greatest admiration for El Greco and if now my admiration is a trifle qualified that is perhaps because I have got out of him all that I am capable of getting. For my own part I find that when a work of art has given me a powerful emotion I cannot recapture it any more than I can eat a dinner I have already eaten. In this I am very unlike a cow. One gets tired of everything. But what remains is the personality behind the work of art; that to some minds is the great interest in the artist's work; and that, so complex is man, is an interest that endures when you know his work by heart.

It is with the personality then of the Greek that I am concerned. There is only one word that I know to describe it and that is one we are told to eschew. The late, but excellent, Fowler tells us that there is no excuse for the use of the word intriguing. He asks plaintively why we should not say interesting or perplexing, but really they do not mean quite the same thing, and if ever

the word is justified it is here. To me it suggests an
ambiguity, a puzzle that invites you to solve it and a
secret that demands all your subtlety to discover it. It is
all very well to tell us that it is formed from the word
intrigue; the adjective has by now acquired a meaning of its own. 1 would say boldly then that no great
artist is more intriguing than El Greco. I have
wondered whether from the little that is known of his
life, from some acquaintance with the circumstances in
which he lived and from his strange and beautiful
paintings, it was possible to get a coherent idea of the
person he was. This indeed was essential if I was in my
pages to draw the portrait of a living man. I thought
also that I might thus explain, at least to my own satisfaction, something of the mysteriousness of his pictures.

Of his life very little is known and that little is
unexpected. Until recently he was thought to have been
born about 1545, or even later, for there is a letter, dated
1570, from Julio Clovio recommending him to the
attention of Cardinal Farnese in which he is described as
a youth; but lately an erudite Spaniard, Don Francisco
San Roman, has proved that he was born in 1541. It
seems strange that Julio Clovio should have called him a
youth when he was hard on thirty; at that time, and
indeed much later, that age was looked upon as the
flower of manhood and youth already passed; but it
agrees well enough with the statement made by Jusepe
Martinez that he died at an advanced age. It is known

that he died in 1614. The explanation may be that Julio Clovio thought thus to excite the sympathy of a possible patron and it may be that, being himself seventy-three, he looked upon a man of thirty as no more than a boy. In his letter he describes him further as a pupil of Titian, and this is at first sight surprising, since the works by which we chiefly know him show the influence of Tintoretto rather than of Titian. But it appears that El Greco's early pictures owe much to him, and the wily Julio Clovio may well have thought it more useful to describe the young man as the pupil of the better known master. He was born in Crete. Of his boyhood nothing is known, but it is supposed that he learnt to paint in the monastery schools in which the manufacture of icons had long been a flourishing industry. He went to Venice, but at what age is uncertain, and after a lengthy sojourn there settled down in Rome. Here he seems to have passed five or six years, and sometime between 1575 and 1577, being then about thirty-five, he went to Spain. He stayed there for the rest of his life. The common view is that in Toledo he recognised his spiritual home. It is held that he acquired his magic colour from the grey walls of that city built upon a rock and from the austere tones of the surrounding country; in his encounter with the Spanish character it is held that he developed an originality that his early works had given small hint of, and in his contact with the passionate Spanish faith achieved the mystical exaltation that inspires his great religious pictures. He has been seen as a man of an austere temper, indifferent to the things of the earth, who went his lonely ascetic way intent only on expressing his rapt vision; and those later pictures of his with their fantastic distortions seemed the final effort to represent a spiritual experience.

This is plausible, romantic enough to please the fancy, and coherent. But it is only credible if you leave out everything that is known of El Greco and that can be seen in his pictures that does not fit in with it. Those cool colours of his were there before ever he went to Spain: it may be that they were the colours he learnt in the Cretan monastery in which he had been taught to paint icons, or it may be that he discovered them in his own sensibility. There is no reason to believe that they would have been different if he had never left Italy. It is singular to find in the portrait of Julio Clovio, painted before his journey to Spain, a landscape with the same tortured sky that he painted so often in his later pictures. It is a sky that in point of fact you do not see in Toledo nearly so often as you do in Venice and indeed you will find it in several of Tintoretto's pictures in the Scuola di San Rocco. In the Madonna del Orto you will find the heavy grey clouds, with their abrupt outlines, looking as though they were cut out of tufa, that are so characteristic of El Greco.

There is no knowing why he went to Spain. It may be

of course that he went because he hoped to get work. Artists were being engaged to decorate the Escorial and a painter who could find little to do at home might well think it worth his while to try his luck abroad. So English actors who cannot get a job in London go to New York and often achieve a success that their own country denied them. A certain Mancini, a contemporary, states that he left Rome because the painters and patrons of the arts resented a remark he had made about Michael Angelo's Last Judgement. The Pope, considering certain figures indecent, desired to have them painted over, whereupon El Greco said that if he would destroy the whole work he would do another, 'not a whit worse than Michelangelo's as a work of art, which would be both chaste and decorous in addition.' Painters must have changed very much since then if they took so much to heart a fellow painter's criticism of a dead painter, and patrons of the arts had much to learn if they attached great importance to what one artist said of another. I can see nothing in El Greco's character to persuade me that any indignation a flout of his might arouse would have driven him from a place he did not want to leave. In a dispute between El Greco and the chapter of Toledo over his picture El Espolio, when asked during the legal proceedings that took place why he had come to Spain, he refused to answer. Considering that he was a foreigner, living among people who did not like foreigners, and at loggerheads with the Church, which few were inclined to affront, it seems strange that he should have declined to give his reason without good cause. It looks very much as though he had something to hide. When you read the novels and biographies of the day it occurs to you how often a journey was occasioned by the tragic outcome of a quarrel. Swords were drawn quickly, often on trivial grounds, and if you were unlucky enough to kill your antagonist it was usual to go while the going was good. I have wondered whether research in the police records of Rome, if such still exist, would not reward the industrious investigator with the explanation why El Greco went to Spain and stayed there. At the same trial he stated that he did not understand Spanish very well. This does not seem to have been questioned. He had then been in Toledo for three or four years. El Greco had provided himself with a sleeping dictionary; which our empire-builders recommend as the best way to acquire the speech of the country they inhabit and so make themselves more competent to bear the white man's burden. He took a mistress, Doña Jeronima de las Cubas, and in 1578, it is supposed, had a son by her. Levantines are quick at learning languages. El Greco's indifference to acquiring Spanish does not look as though he were very much interested in the country which was to be his home for the rest of his life. He never lost his pride in his Greek birth. As is well known he signed his pictures with his full name in Greek characters and added the fact that he

was a Cretan. A list of the books in his possession at his
death has been found. There were about two hundred
of them. Of these only seventeen were in Spanish; but
unfortunately their titles are not given. The rest were
in Italian or Greek. It is hard to resist the conclusion that
his curiosity about Spanish literature was not intense.

Toledo, when El Greco settled there, was no longer
the capital of Spain, but it was still the centre of much
artistic and literary activity. Churches were being built
that had to be decorated. Ecclesiastics lived splendidly.
Poets and dramatists made lengthy sojourns. The
painter might very well have known Lope de Vega and
Cervantes; he certainly knew Gongora, the obscure,
irascible and conceptist poet. Plays were given by
professional actors and by aristocratic amateurs, and
every possible occasion was seized upon, the birth of a
royal prince, the signing of a peace, for splendid
festivities. An attractive picture of the life of the place is
give in the Cigarrales de Toledo to which I have
already referred. It is a dull book, it must be confessed,
and the euphuistic style in which it is written is tedious.
The time of day is told you with such witty conceits that
to discover what it is you need not only some acquaintance with astronomy but also with mythology. When
you are told that a curtain is indebted to the labours of
architectural worms it is easy to guess that it is made of
silk, but you have to think a moment before you
discover that when the author informs you that snow,

transformed into wax by the parturition of the republican, but tiny birds, was burning, he means that the candles were lit. To our modern taste it seems a roundabout way of saying that you threw a letter into the fire unopened to state that only the flames were given leave to unseal it. But for all that you get an impression of leisured, courtly, well-bred persons who took delight in beautiful things. They passed the summer mornings in the pleasures of the chase and fishing (the fish biting with avidity because the bait was offered them by such fair hands); the afternoons in peaceful games, tilting and racing; and the nights in dancing, delectable argument and ingenious devising.

The reader may think that this picture does not correspond very well with what I have said before about the poverty that so constantly oppressed the Spaniards of the Golden Age. Let him go to the Mall on the evening of a Court and look at the long line of cars driving up in which sit dowagers in their diamonds and débutantes in grand new dresses. They tell me that the scene within the Palace is gorgeous beyond description. Then let him stroll along to the Admiralty Arch. He will find a coffee-stall where the hungry are given for nothing a cup of tea and a bite to eat. There he will see a string of men a quarter of a mile long, patiently waiting, one hour, two hours, for the stall to open. He will admit that there is nothing contradictory in what I have said and indeed that it is just what you would expect.

It has been supposed that El Greco lived in the cultured society of the city, consorting with grave ecclesiastics and eminent lawyers; but the only evidence I know of this is that he painted portraits of such personages. He was a man of education and of a pleasant discourse. Among his Greek books, besides classics such as Homer, Euripides, Plutarch and Lucian were the works of certain of the Fathers, St. John Chrysostom, St. Justin, St. Basil; and it is probable that he could converse suitably with the reverend gentlemen who were his principal patrons. Among his Italian books were Petrarch, Ariosto and Bernardo Tasso. In his life, which was described as singular and extravagant, there is nothing to suggest the ascetic. He dwelt in a large house with a display that was thought ostentatious, and he had musicians come from Venice to play to him while he was at dinner. Nothing of this is surprising, for it is an error to suppose that the artist lives in a garret from choice. Philosophers may content themselves with plain living, but painters, writers and musicians are occupied with the things of sense and whenever they have been able, have lived with splendour. They have liked grand houses, with as many servants to wait upon them as they could pay for, and they have seldom hesitated to run into debt to provide themselves with fine clothes. El Greco had a keen eye on the profits of his trade. He made a great deal of money. Of the few documents concerning him that

197

have come down to us several have to do with his quarrels over payment with the patrons who had commissioned him to paint a picture. When the authorities taxed him upon the profits of his work at Illescas he fought them and got a judgement in his favour. So far as I can understand the argument his contention was that what he sold was not canvas and paint, but the art with which he had arranged the paint, and this was not dutiable. Like many another artist before and after him, he was a shrewd business man. He kept in his studio sketches of his pictures so that when the patron came along for an altarpiece he could order what he wanted, a Saint Francis or a Magdalen, an Assumption of the Virgin or Christ bearing the Cross: they were all there, you paid your money and you took your choice. He repeated pictures as often as he was required to. There are two or three versions at least of most of his paintings and of St. Francis in Meditation there are, it appears, over twenty.

There is a peculiar thing about the process of artistic creation which I should not have thought was any different in a painter and a writer. When a writer has been occupied with a subject and has done what he could with it, he is so sick of it that he takes no more interest in it at all. He is like a snake that has sloughed its skin. The subject that has absorbed him ceases to be a part of him; the emotion that filled him when he was working at it is dead and he cannot by any effort of will recapture it. When a writer must take up a theme out of which he has got all he could, making a play out of a novel, to take an example, the labour is mechanical. He cannot expect to have any inspiration. It is a task he performs by exercise of the knowledge he has acquired. I cannot understand how El Greco could have painted the same pictures over and over again if he was really filled with the religious emotion people find in them. I should have thought he could only do this if the subject was of no consequence to him.

The authorities have dealt with this matter in a very simple way. They have divided El Greco's pictures into good, indifferent, and bad. They claim that he painted the good ones by himself, the indifferent with the help of his assistants, who painted the bad ones all by themselves. It seems to me a little too simple. He must have been a very wonderful artist indeed if he never painted a bad picture. It is strange that Tristan, the best of his pupils, when he worked on his own, painted no pictures so good as the worst of those that are with any probability ascribed to his master. Of course El Greco had assistants who prepared the canvas, squared up the design, and presumably did some underpainting; but the contracts that various religious bodies made with him go into such particular detail, they are so careful to state what they want, you cannot persuade yourself that they would have accepted work which they were not reasonably sure was from his own hand.

Indeed when there was a possibility that through death or other hindrance he could not finish a certain work a clause was inserted in the contract that it should be finished by his son Jorge Manuel or by some other specified person. I think some explanation must be sought for the fact that no painter of genius so often repeated his pictures as did El Greco.

Now let us look at the portraits he painted of himself. There is one in the Burial of Count Orgaz and another in the St. Maurizio in the Escorial. It is not certain that they are his portraits, it is only a tradition that they are, but they are evidently portraits of the same man and it is likely that the tradition is true. Accepting them then, on the great authority of Don Manuel Cossio, as authentic I think one may safely say that El Greco may not have looked like this, but this is what he thought he looked like. It is a thin, intelligent face, fresh-coloured, a rather long face; the beard, of a palish, reddish brown, is well trimmed; the hair is dark; the forehead is high and noble; the eyes, somewhat close-set, are cool, observant and reflective. You have the impression of a man who gave a good deal of thought to his appearance. You would have said from the look of him that this was a composed, intelligently curious man, but one capable neither of great passion nor of deep emotion. In neither of these pictures is there in the expression any of the seriousness which one would have thought the occasion demanded. This person seems to preserve a strangely ironic detachment; it would never occur to you that he was a mystic; you might have taken him for a sardonic humorist.

Often the portraits that an artist paints will tell you as much about himself as about his sitters, and I have wondered whether El Greco's would not offer some clue to what I sought. Now when you look at a collection of El Greco's portraits, in the Prado for instance, the first thing that strikes you is their distinction. They have a well-bred elegance. They have gravity and decorum. But it would be absurd to say that they are profound. They seem indeed to be painted in the most perfunctory fashion. The colour is cool and subdued, but no effort is made to use the mass in an effective manner; the bony structure is barely indicated; the heads have no backs to them and the bodies no weight. You get the impression that the Greek was not interested in the people he painted. These men were the contemporaries of the conquistadores and of the saints; they are as empty of character as lord mayors. When you compare these portraits with those of Zurbaran, so actual, so strongly individualized, they cease to exist. More than once certainly El Greco painted a magnificent portrait, but only when some eccentricity in the sitter's appearance gave him the obvious opportunity. Now in fiction it is easy to make a striking character of a person with marked characteristics; the difficulty is to make a man live when he is more or less like everybody else.

Any competent novelist could create the father in the Brothers Karamazov; he needed to be more than that who created the old servant in Un Cœur Simple. I should have thought it was the same in portrait painting. More insight and more imagination were needed, I should have thought, to paint the Man with the Glove than the Grand Inquisitor. It looks as though El Greco regarded his sitters with a singular detachment. Is it possible that this mystic took no interest in the human soul? Though infinitely well-born these people look terribly stupid. They were. The history of Spain during the Golden Age is a history of the abysmal ineptitude of which the human race is capable. A Greek, subtle and quick-witted, a man of culture, it may well be that he was impatient of these fine gentlemen's stupidity.

Years ago I went to Crete, not hoping to find any trace of El Greco, but curious to see the island that had given him birth. From the sea it offers a jagged aspect. It seems to consist of ridge upon ridge of rough, barren and stony hills. Their sharp outlines silhouetted against the sky have an austere and unapproachable beauty. Yet when you go into the interior you find that these hills, tawny, arid and sparsely covered with coarse herbage, separate into pleasing valleys. Here flourish great plantations of ancient olives and in more favourable places vines. Ash-trees and cypresses grow along the streams and oleanders luxuriate at their brim. But when you come away it is not so much the memory of the smiling valleys and the shallow rippling streams that you take with you, but rather of the desolate, wild and tawny hills. When the Greek looked at the gaunt mountain ranges of Castile it must have seemed to him that he was very close to the landscape he had known in childhood.

Candia, outside the main street untidy and bedraggled, is a town of narrow tortuous streets, with low houses that offer a blank wall to the view; and the unpaved road, all holes, is dusty in dry weather and a morass in wet. You might think yourself back in the sixteenth century. By the side of the grand new Greek church is a little old one, very low, dark, and heavy with stale incense. Its reredos is richly carved and gilt and on the walls hang large icons that you can scarcely see. In the sacristy are others. Some of them are very old and one or two are fine. In several a foreign influence is manifest. In them the Byzantine feeling is swamped, but not entirely destroyed, by the easy splendour and the courtly formality of Venetian art. It is not unreasonable to suppose that it was the exciting charm of this new style that impelled the young painter to make his way to Venice.

No one knows how long the Cretan lived in Italy, ten, twelve or fifteen years; but they were the impressionable years of his youth and we know the sort of circumstances he was thrown in. Venice had lost much of its political power and the population was declining, but it was the playground of Europe and life, splendid still, was led by the rich with pomp. Manners were easy, scruples were few. The Bride of the Adriatic resisted as well as she could the efforts of the Papacy to reform her morals and to purify her faith. Thought was free and the intelligent were elegantly sceptical. Rome, alarmed by the Reformation, was making some effort to set her house in order, but there is no evidence that the individual was much inconvenienced by the fervour that reigned in high places. Artists have ever proved hostile to the limitations that puritanism has sought to impose on their private behaviour. From the little that is known of El Greco it seems likely that he would have remained an indifferent spectator of a spiritual movement that his foreign birth made of no great moment to him. Since he died fortified by the rites of the Catholic Church he was presumably received into it, but when you look at his coolly sceptical face you cannot but wonder whether it meant as much to him as those have thought who see in his pictures the most fervent expression of the passion of the Counter-reformation.

Everyone knows how Philip II commissioned El Greco to paint a picture of St. Maurice and his companions for one of the altars of the Escorial and when it was delivered liked it so little that he would not let it be placed in the church but banished it to a cellar. It hangs now in the Sala Capitular and is the greatest glory of the Escorial. In the eyes of the cultured not one of the actions of his long reign has redounded more to the discredit of Philip II. I think he has been harshly treated. He was a sufficiently enlightened patron of the arts to buy the pictures of Titian and to ask Paul Veronese to come to Spain to decorate the stupendous building on which he lavished such vast treasure. He was a deeply and sincerely religious man. He shared the common (and not unreasonable) opinion of his time that saints should be painted in such a manner that one did not lose the desire to pray before them, nay, that they should engender devotion, 'since the chief effect and the end of painting them must be this.' El Greco's picture is of superb vivacity, its colouring is so brilliant and original that the neighbouring pictures look dull be side it; but Philip knew a religious picture when he saw one. In the San Maurizio the three chief figures wear what I suppose are leather jerkins, but they are in effect nudes; their muscles are drawn as in a studio study and even the navels are shown. The angels that fly about the clouds or in easy attitudes rest upon them, playing musical instruments and singing, seem to take part in a divertisement like those prepared by great nobles to honour a royal guest. The figures in the background, the Theban legion, might be stripped for the Olympian games rather than to attest their faith by martyrdom. It would not be strange if Philip was shocked by the frivolity with which El Greco had treated the scene.

The attitude of those various personages is a triumph of elegance. Never did El Greco more obviously paint gestures for their beauty rather than their significance. It is a picture that gives enjoyment; it does not excite devotion.

1 cannot but ask myself why El Greco, who could draw so beautifully when he wanted to, should, apart from his deliberate distortions, at times have drawn so carelessly. Why does he put a Virgin's eye half way down her face or make it pop out of her head as though, poor thing, she had exophthalmic goitre? Why does he sometimes give his saints the look of ducks dying of fright in a thunderstorm? The Virgin in the Crucifixion in the Prado is grotesque; that face would not be out of keeping in a satyric painting by Goya. (But how lovely is the colour, the green tunic worn by St. John, the exquisite tone of the body hanging on the cross, so tender and ethereal, and the richness of that tempestuous sky!) I am tempted to ask myself whether when he painted a religious picture he did not give way sometimes to a sardonic humour. It is difficult to see more than a conventional devotion in those single figures of Franciscan saints which as we know he painted wholesale. The St. Antony in the Prado is composed so perfunctorily that it does not even make sense. In one hand the saint delicately holds a madonna lily, while with the other he supports a heavy open book on which is a small brown object that he seems to study in pitch-black

night; for the background is that stormy sky which El Greco used with amazing pertinacity. And beautiful as I find the Resurrection in the Prado, with the slender, soaring, movingly painted figure; exciting as I find the sweep of those others with their arms raised in such expressive gesture; I am not conscious of any depth of religious feeling. Nor is there any that I can see in the Baptism of Christ. It is a lovely picture, with colour of an intoxicating beauty; those elongated forms, nude but for their loin-cloths, of the Saviour and the Baptist, have an exquisite sophisticated grace; but I feel there no fervour of belief nor rapture of ecstasy. It is disconcerting in that fine picture of Christ bearing the Cross to see the elegance with which the Saviour clasps it. Indeed it is on the hands that El Greco has concentrated the interest. The face, with the eyes showing a great deal of white under the pupil, which was the Cretan's simple way of expressing religious emotion, is the face of a comic actor. Ernest Thesiger might have sat for it. The right hand rests on the cross with the third and fourth fingers together, an old trick of the painter's to get away from the awkwardness of those five odd digits; while the left, again with the third and fourth fingers together, has the little one slightly crooked as ladies of easy virtue to show their refinement crook their little fingers when they drink a glass of champagne.

Not far from the San Maurizio in the Sala Capitular of the Escorial is a picture that portrays religious emotion in a very different manner. It is a Deposition from the Cross, and it is by Van der Weyden. Here the emotion is sincere and natural. The expressions are real. The painter felt what he painted and expressed what he felt. You are moved because he was moved himself. It is an awful moment that is represented and there is a sense of despair in the droop of those figures that makes you feel that here is the most terrifying moment in the world's history. The men are stricken with grief, but gravely masters of it; Mary has swooned and there is another woman, Mary Magdalen, I suppose, whose clumsy, broken attitude gives you a tragic impression of hopelessness. All these people feel as they would feel and act as they would act. It is a beautiful picture, a terrible scene, and one to bring home to a rude and brutal people the horror of the event represented. Its sincerity is shattering. You cannot look at it and again believe in El Greco's religious sense.

I do not doubt that he was one of the greatest painters that ever lived. I think the Burial of Count Orgaz is one of the greatest pictures in the world. It has a sweep, a freshness and a vitality that are amazing. It fills you with stupefaction. El Greco was a master of gesture. You would never think that an outflung arm, a raised hand, a foot on tip-toe or an extended leg, could have such a miraculous grace. He had indeed a wonderful sense of the beautiful though limited gestures permitted to the hand. The general effect of a large number of his pictures together, as you may see them in the room in the Prado, is thrilling; it is not only that distinguished, cool yet not cold, colour that moves you, but something in the pictures themselves, apart also from their subjects, their form and architecture. It is something troubling, sinister and enigmatic; I can only suppose it is the personality of the painter. It is like looking into the darkness of a lake in the mountains. You feel vaguely scared. You wonder whether there is anything there at the bottom, a secret that it would be good for you to know, or whether it is an aimless depth that has no purpose. For depth in itself has no greater significance than breadth. The lake may look bottomless only because it is muddy, and if you take a header into it you can easily crack your skull. In literature, I know, the obscure is very often taken for the profound. Here, however, time plays an odd trick; it dissipates obscurity as a breeze dissipates fog, and then are discovered, not the great truths we hoped for, but painted trifles. Thus time has made most of Mallarmé's poems quite clear and we see that all that labyrinthine imagery hid from the vulgar nothing more abstruse than the poetic commonplaces of the day. All that remains to delight us is a number of pellucid and beautiful phrases.

It gives you a curious sensation to go from the room in which the El Grecos are hung into the Velasquez room next door. It is like coming into the warm light of common day. You cannot but feel that Velasquez is somewhat superficial, but he is superficial on the grand scale. He had an equable, sunny temperament and his pictures are delightfully gay. He had that alegria which is the Andalusian's most cherished and characteristic grace. He does not in his portraits suggest a criticism of his sitters. He takes them at their face value. He was the greatest of court-painters. His charm was combined with a genial heartlessness. His dwarfs and fools are painted with amusement. So might Shakespeare have drawn them. He had no feeling for the horror of their deformity or the misery of their lot. His cheerful temper enabled him to look upon these loathsome abortions with the good humour of one who knew that the Almighty had created them to be the playthings of princes. I suppose no one can deny his miraculous skill in painting, the silvery lustre of his blacks and the richness of his sober tones. He could paint the dress of an infanta in such a manner as to take one's breath away. But even as one admires one is filled with a slight sense of uneasiness and one asks oneself whether this wonderful skill is worth while. It reminds one of a writer who says things with exquisite sobriety, but says nothing of any great consequence. But how skilfully these figures are placed on the canvas to make a pattern pleasing to the eye! In the full length of Philip IV with his gun and in the companion picture of the Cardinal-Infante pure representation seems to achieve perfect beauty. There is nothing to be said. You can only stand and gape.

When you go back to the El Greco room you enter a troubled world. Here is a wild intensity that seems to seek utterance for no emotion that can be made clear by symbols. It is a vague and tormenting sensation that seems to oppress him, like that anxiety, common at times to us all, I suppose, to which no cause can be assigned; you do not know whether it is of the body or the spirit. It was not a man of equable and sunny temper who painted these pictures, but a man of uncertain humour perplexed by fantastic longings; it was a man striving with pain for an expression that he sought in the abyss of his soul as though it were a memory hovering just below consciousness that it exasperated him to be unable to recall. But if he was a mystic his mysticism must surely be sought in another sphere than the religious. Pacheco, who saw him in his old age, says of El Greco that he was a great philosopher, very witty in his speech, personal, profound, with an original answer to everything. We know that he was luxurious and improvident; indeed he died insolvent; the portraits he painted of himself suggest scepticism and irony; and one's own sensibility persuades one that he was very lonely. Even in Rome he had a high conceit of himself and later on his arrogance was overweening. In the action over his remuneration for the Burial of Count Orgaz he finished his pleadings with the words: 'as true as it is that the payment is inferior to the value of my sublime work, my name will pass to posterity, which will recompense my work and glorify the author as one of the greatest geniuses of Spanish painting.' He was a Levantine and the Levantines are apt to express themselves with grandiloquence. No writer can have gone to Alexandria or Beyrout without being visited by some young author who tells him in bad but fluent French that he has written a novel vastly better than anything that Balzac, Anatole France or—Zola ever wrote. It is a bombastic use of words that does not preclude a real and often touching modesty. But humility is the very substance of the soil on which religious mysticism grows and it would be absurd to say that El Greco had it. There is a story which, if true, shows that he was something of an actor and the art of bluff was not unfamiliar to him. The story runs as follows: Tristan, his pupil, had painted for a stipulated price a picture for the Jeronimite monks of the convent of Sisla, but when the picture was finished the monks (doubtless with justice) thought it was not worth it and wanted to pay less. The matter was submitted to the arbitration of El Greco. He looked at the picture and then, flying into a passion, began to beat Tristan with his stick. The monks interposed. 'Tristan is but young,' they said, 'and does not understand that he is asking too much.' 'Too much!' cried El Greco. 'It is a sublime and beautiful work and I am beating him for daring to ask two hundred ducats for a picture that is worth five hundred, and if you don't pay the money at once I'm going to take it myself.' The monks paid.

Taking it all in all you have the impression of a man who possessed most of the traits that we generally hold to be typical of the Levantine, and if you combined these ingeniously I do not think it would be impossible to construct an image coherent enough to be credible. The various particulars fit like the pieces of a jig-saw puzzle. The flaw lies in the fact that there is nothing in the sort of man you have thus created to account for the pictures he painted. One must look further.

Not long ago I came across the suggestion, made in a ribald spirit, that El Greco was homosexual. I have thought it worth considering. So far as an artist's work is concerned there is as a rule little interest in knowing about his sexual life, upon which indeed an exaggerated stress is generally laid. There is a notion that men who have in any way greatly distinguished themselves should in this respect be different from their fellows, and when the student discovers that they have had love affairs he is apt to think the fact strangely significant. For all the to-do that has been made over the amours of Shelley and Byron I cannot but doubt whether they were very different from those of other young men of their class. Many a smart young broker in the City of London would have looked upon them with supercilious amusement as extremely meagre. But when it comes to an abnormality the case is different. I have suggested that talent consists in an individual way of seeing the world combined with a natural aptitude for creation and that genius is talent with a greater capacity and a universal sympathy. Now it cannot be denied that the homosexual has a narrower outlook on the world than the normal man. In certain respects the natural responses of the species are denied to him. Some at least of the broad and typical human emotions he can never experience. However subtly he sees life he cannot see it whole. If it were not for the perplexing sonnets I should say that the homosexual can never reach the supreme heights of genius. I cannot now help asking myself whether what I see in El Greco's work of tortured fantasy and sinister strangeness is not due to such a sexual abnormality as this. I hasten to add that this can be nothing but surmise, as is all else I have said of him. Besides his pictures, the letter of Julio Clovio, certain legal documents, his death certificate and the list of his effects there is no material for any direct knowledge of him. Whatever does not proceed from this, however confidently it is stated, can be no more than plausible.

When you survey possibilities it must be admitted that there is in this one a good deal that saves it from being wildly improbable. El Greco spent his childhood and youth in places where he can have conceived no instinctive aversion to that idiosyncrasy. I should say that a distinctive trait of the homosexual is a lack of deep seriousness over certain things that normal men take seriously. This ranges from an inane flippancy to a sardonic humour. He has a wilfulness that attaches importance to things that most men find trivial and on the other hand regards cynically the subjects which the common opinion of mankind has held essential to its spiritual welfare. He has a lively sense of beauty, but is apt to see beauty especially in decoration. He loves luxury and attaches peculiar value to elegance. He is emotional, but fantastic. He is vain, loquacious, witty and theatrical. With his keen insight and quick sensibility he can pierce the depths, but in his innate frivolity he fetches up from them not a priceless jewel but a tinsel ornament. He has small power of invention, but a wonderful gift for delightful embroidery. He has vitality, brilliance, but seldom strength. He stands on the bank, aloof and ironical, and watches the river of life flow on. He is persuaded that opinion is no more than prejudice. In short he has many of the characteristics that surprise us in El Greco. It may be that in this abnormality lies the explanation why his pictures fail of that ultimate greatness which is release. They thrill; they do not give you peace. They excite; but do not satisfy. We know that whatever imagination El Greco had he did not apply it to the composition of his pictures. The learned have traced the patterns of some of them to the Byzantine icons with which he may be presumed to have been familiar in his early youth and of others to pictures he had seen in Italy. It is curious that in the full flush of his early manhood, when fancy is generally exuberant, he should have been content so often to take his designs from the woodcuts, engravings and etchings that were at that time current articles of commerce in Italy. When he had to invent something out of his head he was not remarkable. The Burial of Count Orgaz betrays its Byzantine inspiration. A dozen artists in Italy could have arranged it on a more satisfactory plan. It is only the miraculous painting that prevents that row of heads, cutting the picture into two parts, from being disconcerting. And when he had to represent the martyrdom of St. Maurice he shirked it and painted a group of young men who might be discussing the handicapping for the school sports. There is in Toledo a San Bernardino, with a tiny head, a courtly little pointed beard and an immensely long body against a gloomy sky, which is quite charming; but in the same way as the twisted pillars of a plateresque patio are charming. It is a delicious picture for a great lady's oratory. But it could hardly arouse devotion. It is perfectly frivolous. I think no religious painter ever expressed emotion so perfunctorily as El Greco. This would not be strange if he were entirely devoid of it.

A little while ago, confessing a former error, I made a

distinction between the artist's work from his creative standpoint and its communication, which is what the layman is concerned with. I think a good deal of criticism is rendered less illuminating than it should be because critics often do not clearly distinguish between the two. They step from one to the other without realising that they are doing so. There need be no relation between them. The artist is not justified in claiming to be judged from the standpoint of his intention. That is important to him, and to anyone who cares to study his personality, but it is of no importance to the observer. The artist is driven to produce by an instinct within him that impels him to express his personality. He does not try to do this; it is an inevitable accident that he does so. He is in all probability not very much interested in his personality. (I am not speaking of the journeyman who busies himself with the arts to earn an honest living or the spent worker who continues to do so from habit.) The artist can no more help creating than water can help running down hill. It is a release from the burden on his soul. It is a spiritual exercise which is infinitely pleasurable, and it is accompanied by a sense of power that is in itself delightful. When production fulfils it he enjoys a heavenly sense of liberation. For one delicious moment he rests in a state of equilibrium. What the painter paints or the writer writes is an experience of himself and the theorists of art for art's sake were right when they claimed that it had no moral value. Nor need this experience and its expression, whatever its importance for the person who feels it, have any value for anybody else. That must depend on the interest for the world of the personality that has thus been forced to exteriorise itself.

I think there are two ways in which El Greco sought deliverance. One was in decoration. To my mind he was singularly indifferent to his subjects. They were given him and like all artists he worked out his own intentions within the limitations imposed upon him by the circumstances of his time. That is why he could paint the same picture over and over again. These saints, Francis or Antony, meant no more to him than did their abstract designs to the early cubists. To him they were merely excuses for his decorative inventions. And that is why he was so much more interested in the hand than in the head. The hand has a possibility of lovely gesture that is denied to the head. No one has painted hands more exquisitely. But in many of the pictures they are placed with such an affected grace that, considering the episode represented, you are shocked by the unseemliness. El Greco was ready to sacrifice truth of gesture to beauty of attitude. His reaction was, in short, baroque.

The reader must pardon me if I indulge now in a short disquisition on baroque. I do this not only because I think the subject in itself interesting, but because I seem to discern in that form of art and the circumstances that brought it about much that corresponds with the art of the present day and the conditions in which we are now living. I suppose everyone is agreed that massivity and movement are the essentials of baroque. It used decoration, not to complete a composition, but for its own sake; and its wonderful discovery was that movement was decorative. The spectacular nature of architecture has caused the learned to study baroque particularly in that art. This has made it a little more difficult to discover its distinctive features. The decorative element is not so noticeable in a building because the architect has made it for a certain use and this use conditions his treatment. But when you look more closely you cannot but see how much these great artists were concerned with it. They aimed at unity, whereas the Renaissance architects were content to make a harmonious composition of self-subsisting parts; and unity of effect is the first demand of decoration. We hesitate when we are told that the baroque architects sought to represent movement and our inclination is to think that they were aiming at something foreign to the spirit of their art and therefore necessarily bad. The play they made with light and shade seems like a device to deceive the eye into accepting what is contrary to nature. It takes a little while to recognise that mass is but an instant in the unending curve of movement. It is not my business here to point out the various uses they made of the expedients at their command and the triumphant success with which they achieved their ends. But the sway of baroque was by no means confined to architecture; it affected the painters and sculptors too, the writers, and I should imagine the musicians. Indeed I suspect that it gave their art for the first time the possibility of reaching the cloud-capt heights which Beethoven and Wagner attained. But of music I know nothing. I went to Cambridge to ask a great authority whether there was anything in my surmise, but thinking perhaps that it was no affair of mine he would not tell me.

Baroque is often considered to be the characteristic expression of the Counter-reformation. It seems unlikely that it was created by it. The Counter-reformation built new churches and restored old ones. The artists who worked in them were baroque artists. They were sentimental, violent and theatrical as was the religion of the period, but not necessarily on account of it. Religion was declamatory; it exaggerated the manifestations of its piety in reaction from the pagan scepticism of the Renaissance and in challenge to the Lutheran strenuousness. It suited very well the new style the artists were now making use of; the extravagant emotions they were asked to express gave them an opportunity to use movement for purely decorative purposes and movement they could only represent by mass. I should have said that the Counter-reformation, so far as it was not dictated by fear, corresponded to a feeling that was in the air and it was this feeling that created the universal tendency towards the baroque.

It is interesting to consider why this absorption in decoration, which to my mind is the essence of the style, should just at this time have made itself felt. Some writers have ascribed it to a normal reaction from the preceding period. The Renaissance was over and people were tired of the works it had produced. That was very natural, for man desires change and he wearies even of perfection. Beauty is a full stop and when you have reached it you can do nothing but start another sentence. The inspiration that the discovery of the antique had brought was exhausted. But boredom with one style cannot give rise to another; a new style arises from a new state of the spirit.

The Renaissance cultivated measure and repose. It cherished the golden mean. Its strength was tranquil. Art not only occupied an important part in men's lives, but the artists felt themselves in conformity with the life about them. They were citizens of the state as well as artists. Sin was original sin and the individual did not feel himself answerable for it. Man was free, if not always in fact, in imagination. And freedom was the most cherished of his ideals.

But the attempt to think again the thoughts and live once more the life enshrined in the literatures of Greece and Rome failed. Liberty died. Half of Italy was in the hands of Spain and the rest in the power of petty tyrants. The Inquisition, fostered by the Spanish kings as an instrument of state, acquired a new power in Italy. Incidents here and there in the picaresque novels prove the terror it inspired. Catholicism was restored by force. The Church claimed control over all the activities of the human mind, its philosophy, its science and its art. A strange disquiet oppressed the spirits of men. It seemed as though in their long struggle with intellect they had grown exhausted. Believers, notwithstanding, were uneasy, and they drowned their hesitations in a sea of declamation. They were intolerant because they were afraid. Man was deprived of his inalienable right of self-realisation and freedom was lost to him it seemed for ever.

Freedom is man's greatest good. When you rob the artist of this you force him back upon himself. When he can no longer deal with the great issues of life that in happier times occupy the souls of men, his instinct of creation, which nevertheless demands expression, can but turn to decoration. When men are wretched they look into their hearts and some inexplicable instinct leads them to ascribe their misery to their own shortcomings. Their minds turn to another world and they look for solace to their vexed spirits in the eternal. Sin was no longer original sin; it was personal, and a rigid reckoning would be demanded of the sinner. Decoration with its vague meanings can very well express the desire for the unearthly, the vague fear and the sense of guilt that haunted the souls of men to whom the healthy and inspiring activity of free men was denied. The Renaissance, essentially objective, copied and idealised nature; but baroque used nature as a vehicle to display its own morbid sensibility. It was subjective. And the most direct expression of the subjective is decoration. It is worth while to consider for a moment how the writers reacted to the conditions in which they found themselves. They turned away from matter and busied themselves with form. They sought brilliant and exquisite conceits, no matter how frivolous, and put them in the manner most calculated to surprise. They cultivated rhetoric, the play upon words, flowers of speech, archaisms and such-like toys. They wanted to show their cleverness rather than to discover their hearts. All artists have in them something of the child. They like to play and if they lack serious and great convictions are very likely to squander their faculties on spiritual kickshaws. They do not try to make bread without leaven; they try to make bread with nothing but leaven. Michael Angelo, resuming in himself the restlessness and dissatisfaction of the age, tried by vastness, by violence, to express the passion of his tortured heart, and so became in the plastic arts the father of baroque. His contemporaries and successors felt the significance of what he had invented. Realising quickly the immense decorative value of mass and movement they began with growing assurance to make them the principles of their activity. But because they lacked his spiritual power their works seldom achieved his complete sincerity; and decoration, which had been grave and sincere because it corresponded to a deep instinct in the artist's nature, degenerated with time to the frivolous ornament of rococo.

Now let me return to El Greco. There was in him to my mind a temper that exactly suited the spirit that he found prevalent to some extent in Venice, and at its height in Rome. So he became the greatest of baroque painters. Looking at the whole series of his pictures I seem to see his interest in decoration for decoration's sake grow in intensity. His contemporaries thought that he painted in an increasingly fantastic manner because he went mad. I do not believe it. More recently it has been suggested that he suffered from astigmatism and it has been said that if you put on the right glasses his vertiginous figures would assume normal proportions. I do not believe it. Their immense elongation, which, I may remind the reader, he will find also in many of Tintoretto's pictures, seems to me a natural development of treating the human form as decoration. Because El Greco was aiming at this and nothing else I think he grew more and more indifferent to fact. This, I think, explains also his cock-eyed virgins. If the body, with its mass, is treated as a unit of expression the face becomes of no importance. It is not strange that the moderns should have set such great store by El Greco. If he were alive to-day I imagine he would paint pictures as abstract as the later work of Bracque, Picasso and Fernand Léger. And it may be that the interest in formal design of the present day is due to the same causes as produced baroque art in the sixteenth century. Now too we are spiritually at sixes and sevens. Afraid of the sublime, we take refuge in the multiplication table.

For now the world is sullen and jealous as was the world of the Counter-reformation. The great issues that occupied the Victorians, which seemed to offer the spirit boundless horizons, have played us false. We mock at those who maunder of truth, goodness and beauty. We are afraid of greatness. And we too have lost the inestimable blessing of freedom. Liberty throughout the world is dying or dead. Like the Jesuit novice who lost his personality to find it again in the Company we are asked to surrender our own to find it again in the State. Nobody dares tackle great subjects and the heresy has become orthodox that subject is of no consequence. Only the pretty, the ingenious, the amusing are cultivated. Artists have not yet learnt how to deal with what really matters to our world and so are driven to devote themselves to decoration. They make technical devices the end and aim of their endeavour. They have cast off the shackles of tradition, but use their independence to stand on their heads and, like

Hippokleides, kick their legs in the air. Modern critics are wrong when they blame writers for writing about themselves. When art is no more than a side issue they have nothing else to write about.

But of course there is more in El Greco than the fantastic patterns he devised, his grace and distinction, the elegance of his gestures and his dramatic intensity, seldom falling into theatricalism, with which as I take it he satisfied the sardonic, ironic, sumptuous, sinister side of his nature. When you see many of a painter's pictures together you find in them often a certain monotony. An artist can only give you himself and he is unfortunately always very like himself. The startling thing about El Greco is that, such is his vitality, he can under the most unlikely conditions give you an impression of variety. Take for instance that collection of the Apostles which is in what is now called la casa del Greco. They are three-quarter lengths, canvases of the same size, and the personages are not happily individualised; but the vigour with which they are painted makes them lively and different. You feel in them the stubborn idiosyncrasy of their creator, in wonderful possession of his faculties, who, regardless of what people thought, was getting marvellous satisfaction out of their exercise. Then there is his colour. This, I think, was the second of the two methods by which he strove to release his spirit from its burden; and it is his colour that makes him so wonderful an artist. A

painter thinks with his brushes. Such thoughts as he has
that can be put into words are for the most part commonplace. Why artists are often incomprehensible to other
people is that they express their profoundest feelings
in a language of their own. I think El Greco put the
most serious emotion of his strange, perhaps inexplicable personality into the colours that he set down
on canvas. However he acquired his palette, he gave
it an intensity, a significance, which were his own.
Colour was his complete and unique experience. They
are not so far wrong who see in him a mystic, though
I cannot help thinking that to look upon him as a
religious mystic is superficial. If mysticism is that state
that renders you conscious of depths of truth unknown
to the intellect, revealing like 'glimpses of forgotten
dreams' a greater significance in life and union with
some larger reality, then I think you can hardly fail to
find it in El Greco's painting. I seem to see as great
a mystic rapture in the painting of the right side of the
body of Christ in the Crucifixion in the Louvre as in
any of the experiences of Santa Teresa.

XI

NO one can travel through the various paths of the Spanish scene in the sixteenth century without getting a frequent glimpse of that mysticism that seems to dwell only just below the threshold of consciousness in so many of these passionate men who, you would have thought, were completely immersed in the turmoil of the world. In Spain you are seldom long out of sight of the mountains. They rise before you, arid, gaunt and austere; blue on the far horizon, they seem to summon you to a new and magic world. The Sierra Nevada with its mantle of snow is remote and formidable, but in the dawn or at sunset shines with a coloured beauty not of this earth. And so mysticism, never very far away, unobtrusive but insistent, with its strange attraction that all the human in you resists, seems to haunt the shadows that darken the brilliant prospect. It is like a troubling, tragic and lovely theme that runs through a florid symphony. It is disconcerting and yet you cannot but attend to it.

The idea I had in mind did not allow me to neglect a phase that seemed to me so characteristic of the life

I was studying, but I was conscious that I must tread warily. They say that to understand mysticism you must be a mystic, as to understand love you must be a lover. And Catholic mysticism demands a belief in certain affirmations that many of us find it impossible to accept. This is not the place for me to say what my own beliefs are in the matters with which religion deals, but it is only proper that I should state my conviction that no one of the faiths that men have embraced is ample enough to account for the enormous mystery. They seem to me like blind alleys cut into a primeval jungle and man deceives himself when he thinks they can lead him to its heart.

I think the mystic is in error when he regards mysticism as essentially religious. I do not think religious mysticism is its only form; I should hesitate even to admit that it was its highest. If the mystical experience is a liberating sense of community with what for want of a better word we name reality, and this you can call as you will the Absolute or God, then at some time we are all in greater or less degree mystics. Did not Plotinus say that the power of spiritual intuition was a faculty that all possess, though few use? The sap of the Mystic Vine may be set flowing in more ways than one. The mystical experience is an awareness of a greater significance in the universe, 'other than the known and above the unknown,' a dissolution of the self into a wider self; and this is accompanied by a great rush of vitality, a feeling of power, a sense of union with God or nature, and a strangely exhilarating feeling that depths upon depths of truth are within one's grasp. It is an ecstasy. But you can get it, if you are that way inclined, from a glass of cold beer, from the sight of a well-remembered scene, from opium, from love, by prayer and fasting and mortification of the flesh, and if you are an artist in the excitement of creation.

It is a natural, though unreasonable, instinct to judge of the value of a thing by its origin, and it is hard to accept the fact that the ecstasy that may be aroused in a weary man from drinking a glass of beer can have as much worth as that of the monk in his cell when a divine rapture rewards his long vigil and urgent prayer. But the ecstasy is the same and its value lies in its results. On this point all the mystics are agreed. St. Teresa, tormented by the fear that her experiences were the work of the devil, states that the only test is the effect they have. The mystical experience is valuable only if it strengthens the character and enables him who has enjoyed it to do great things.

The Spanish mystics, the only ones I know at first hand, and that I must admit but inadequately, are not, if I may say so, lively reading. Spanish writers have never cultivated the austere virtue of concision and when they deal with religious subjects feel no call to check their verbosity. They write, not to entertain the reader, but to the glory of God; and it is perhaps natural for them to suppose that they achieve this object more nobly by dissertations of great length. The mystics suffer also from the disadvantage that they all have very much the same thing to say. Their peculiar experience seems to each of them extremely important, as indeed it is, but it is not sufficiently different from mystic to mystic to make it easy to peruse with patience the various accounts. On one occasion I found myself in foreign parts with the complete works of St. Teresa and nothing much else that I wanted to read at the moment, so with the exception of one or two short pieces that were too ejaculatory for my taste I read them all. Though doubtless I did not obtain from them the spiritual edification I might have, they gave me a great deal of enjoyment. The critics say she was a careless writer, but she always managed to get into her writing that sound of the living voice that we all, for the most part without success, aim at; and there was nothing she wrote in which she failed to display her vivacious, charming, wilful, spirited and determined character. She was, if not a great, a grand woman. Maria de San José describes her as of medium height, but on the tall side. In her youth she was thought beautiful and she retained traces of good looks to the end of her life. Her face was neither round nor long, her brow broad and comely; the eyebrows were thick and arched, of a reddish colour; her eyes black and vivacious, not very large but well placed in her face. She was of good proportions, stout rather than slender, and her hands were small and shapely. She was not indifferent to her looks, indeed she accused herself of the fault in confession, and when Fray Juan de la Miseria did a portrait of her she cried, on looking at it: 'God forgive you for having painted me, Brother John, for you have painted me ugly and blear-eyed.'

The life that St. Teresa wrote of herself is one of the great autobiographies of the world. It does not stand too far below the Confessions of St. Augustine. She wrote her more important works only at the command of her confessors, but when you read her life you can hardly resist the conviction that it would have been a very subtle confessor who avoided commanding her to do what she had set her heart on. One of the greatest mercies vouchsafed to her took the form of private communication from the Lord, in which for the most part he ordered her to do what she had very much a mind to. He even enjoined her to write down his observations so that men might profit by them, though some must have offended her deep humility and others to the modern reader must seem a trifle lacking in piquancy. It hardly needed a voice from heaven to tell us that true security consists in the testimony of a good conscience. It is perhaps a little unexpected to hear the Lord apprising St. Teresa of the fact that it was the devil who had caused the Lutherans to remove the images from their churches in order to deprive them of the possibility of correcting their errors, from which ensued that they were all damned. Once indeed he gave her an assurance which the event so little substantiated that one can only imagine that omnipotence sometimes takes a rest. For the Lord told St. Teresa that Father Jeronimo Gracian, a confessor for whom she had a particular attachment, was his real son and that he would never cease to help him. She could hardly have anticipated from this that his life would be one of extreme vexation. He got on the wrong side of most of the people he had to do with and was forced to resign pretty well every appointment his talents secured him. He was clapped into the prison of his monastery by direction of his superiors and finally expelled from his order. He was rejected by all the other orders that he tried to enter. He was captured by Turks, branded with red-hot irons, loaded with chains and thrown into an underground dungeon where he was given black and verminous bread to eat and water to drink so foul that none could have drunk it unless he were dying of thirst. Seldom indeed has the rod been so little spared.

St. Teresa offers the best account that for my part I have read of the various steps of the Mystic Way, and since its main lines can be given very briefly I hope the reader will forgive me if I here state them. The first stage is called Purgation and in this the Soul, aware of Divine Beauty, realises its own nothingness. By prayer and mortification it prepares itself for the second stage of Illumination. In this the Soul begins to recollect itself and touches the supernatural. St. Teresa calls it the Prayer of Quiet. It is a period of rich contemplation. The faculties are not lost, neither do they sleep, but they are gathered up within the soul; and only the will is alive. And the will surrenders itself to God. It desires nothing and asks nothing. Some reach this. Few pass beyond. The third stage is the state of Union and this is the goal of the Mystic Way. It is a glorious folly, a heavenly madness, says the saint, in which is learnt true wisdom, and it is an exquisite enjoyment of the soul. It offers peace, strength and certainty. But it is impossible to explain. 'He that has experienced it will understand something of it, for it cannot be told more clearly, since what here occurs is so obscure. All I can say is that one feels that one is joined with God, and so great a certainty of this remains that in no way can one cease to believe it.'

But St. Teresa never lost her fear that these states of the soul might be inspired by the evil one and she sought constant reassurance from her confessors. She was suspicious of such experiences when they occurred to the nuns under her charge. When she spoke of those moments of ecstasy, when the soul losing consciousness was seized by the rapture of the Divine Vision, she did not fail to add a warning: 'this is the end of that spiritual union,' she told the nuns, 'that there may be born of it works, works.'

It is now that one is inclined to pause. For as everyone knows the saint's great achievement was the reform of the Order of Carmel. Starting with one small convent at Avila she presently founded houses both for men and women in other places. I have always been a little sorry for the poor nuns on whom her zeal forced a stricter rule. It is true that they no longer fasted, as they had originally done, from Holy Cross Day till Easter, nor lived in perpetual solitude; visitors were allowed and the nuns were permitted to leave the precincts of their house. But it must be remembered that the conventual life was adopted in Spain at that period for motives that were not exclusively religious. The entail of estates on eldest sons forced the younger ones either to enter the army or the church, and in the humbler ranks of society the church offered clever men their only chance of advancement. The times were insecure and means of livelihood hard to come by. The cloister promised safety and at least bed and board. Trade was disastrous and those engaged in it were despised. It was only natural that men should put their sons to a calling that kept them alive and was honourable besides. Nor was it always an urgent devotion that led women to the nunnery. Great gentlemen often could not give their daughters a dowry sufficient to marry them suitably and the convent was a dignified way of disposing of them. With the wars in Flanders and the attraction of the Indies men were scarce and many women had no chance of marrying. The convent was their refuge. It offered the disconsolate widow a respectable retreat from the temptations to which her condition was liable. It was the refuge also of girls whose reputation had by their own fault or by an accident been tarnished, and the faintest breath of suspicion was enough to sully a Spanish woman's delicate honour. The reader will remember the Mayor of Zalamea's sardonic remark, 'the Lord is not fastidious of the quality of his brides.' In fact there were a dozen reasons for a woman to enter a religious house other than the love of God. Sometimes they were communities engaged in a particular handicraft and you went to the convent as you might go to a shop. It is not astonishing if these women, performing their duties with sufficient exactitude, sought such alleviations as they could get for a life that only a perfervid piety could save from being very monotonous. They were simple and industrious; they fed the poor who came to their gates, and if they were not more than reasonably pious, they were harmless. It was always possible even in these circumstances for a nun to lead a life devoted entirely to prayer and mortification. It is no wonder that considerable resistance was set up when Teresa de Jesus sought to restore her order to its primitive severity.

There was a plague of nuns and monks in Spain. Whole families entered the church; of the five brothers and sisters of the Jesuit Baltasar Gracian, all but one who died young were members of a religious order. To save his soul was in the sixteenth century the main business of a Spaniard. It has been reckoned that thirty per cent of the population were in the church. Not only were politicians and economists alarmed, but the clergy themselves. The authorities of Madrid and Toledo petitioned for a reduction of the number of religious and the Bishop of Badajoz noted the abundance of convents as one of the ills that were ruining the country. To their number then St. Teresa, regardless of everything but salvation, added. Her fame and the attraction for the Spanish character of the austerity of the rule led many who would otherwise have been content with the life of the world to take the vows. With the growing distress of the country the Lord was providing for his brides with increasing inadequacy; it was all very well to look upon privation as a mortification pleasing in his sight, but the poor nuns were obliged to eat to keep body and soul together and in certain convents they were just dying of hunger. The bishops were in consequence determined that no religious house should be founded unless it was properly endowed. They frowned on the fancy to set up houses of their own that nuns of position or character sometimes took. But the bishops were no match for Teresa de Jesus. With the prestige of her visions and the Redeemer's very words to support her she got as usual her own way. The order was divided and the Discalced Carmelites formed into a distinct province. The energetic saint founded no less than thirty-two houses. Her nuns lived entirely upon alms. They were to have no income, the Lord would provide; and in the Constitutions (a document very revealing of her character) she lays down that if there was food it should be eaten at eleven in winter and at ten in summer; but that no regular hour could be fixed, for it must depend upon what the Lord gave. It may be that St. Teresa's example was salutary to many and that a number of religious who followed her rule found salvation, but it can hardly be denied that her activity assisted in the ruin of her unhappy country.

But none of this is very much to my purpose. I have been seduced into writing this short piece by the interest which, as a novelist, I have not been able to help feeling in her curious personality. She was not, I think, a woman of remarkable intelligence but she had charm, determination and courage. These are the traits that effect great things in the world. They do not always effect wise ones.

In the Book of the Foundations, a work rich in entertainment, full of good sense, humour and curious anecdote, there is a charming account of the founding of a convent at Salamanca. St. Teresa, accompanied only by Sister Mary of the Sacrament, arrived there on the Eve of All Souls about midday after travelling great part of the night in excessive cold. She was in poor health. From the inn she sent for a good man, Nicolas

Gutierrez, whom she had entrusted with the work of making a house ready for her. It had been no easy matter to get it, since it was not the season for letting houses and it was in possession of a number of students who were most unwilling to leave. Nicolas Gutierrez told her that the house was not yet empty, for he had been unable to get the students out. The good mother told him how important it was for her to move in at once, so he went to the landlord and so arranged things that it was empty by evening. But when the two nuns were able to go in it was dusk. The students had left the house in bad order, and so dirty that they had not a little work to do that night. It was large and rambling, with many garrets, and Mary of the Sacrament, more timorous than her stout-hearted Superior, could not get the students out of her thoughts. They had been so loth to go she was afraid some of them might still be hiding in the house. The women shut themselves up in a room with straw in it, 'that being the first thing I provided for founding the house, for with straw we could not fail to have a bed.' The fathers of the Company of Jesus had lent them a couple of blankets. When the door was safely closed Sister Mary seemed somewhat more at her ease about the students, but she kept looking about her first on this side and then on that.

'I asked her why she was looking about, seeing that no one could possibly come in,' says Teresa.

'She replied: "Mother, I am thinking, if I were to

die now what would you do by yourself?" '

Teresa could not help thinking it would be a horrible thing. She was a little startled, because though she did not actually fear dead bodies they made her nervous, even when there was someone with her. But she answered:

'Sister, should that happen I will think what to do. Now let me go to sleep.'

As they had spent two bad nights, sleep soon put an end to their tremors. Next morning mass was said in that house for the first time. But Teresa could never afterwards think of Sister Mary's trepidation without wanting to laugh.

Yes, a woman of character.

It is character too that makes Fray Luis de Leon a fascinating subject and in his case I feel that I have some justification for dwelling upon him for a little. He died in 1591, so the hero of my book could hardly have listened to his lectures, but I like to think that when he was studying at Salamanca he might have come in contact with the young Augustinian whom in Los Nombres de Cristo, Fray Luis calls Juliano and from him heard something of the master of Spanish prose.

Salamanca is an agreeable place to linger in. It has a noble square, with arches all round it, and here towards evening the whole population perambulates, the men in one direction, the girls in the other, so that they may ogle one another as they pass. The town-hall, with its plateresque facade, is rose-coloured. The mass of the cathedral seen from a little distance is fine; it seems to be planted on the ground with a sort of solid arrogance; but when you approach you are repelled by its ugly reddish brown and the florid decoration. The interior is overwhelmingly magnificent. There are huge, lofty pillars that tower to a height that seems hardly believable. The choir is surrounded by elaborate bas-reliefs. It is all so grand and sumptuous, it reminds you of a Lord Mayor's banquet; it suggests a ceremonial, assured, opulent religion, and you ask yourself what solace in trouble the stricken heart could hope to find there.

At the University, sadly fallen from its ancient glory, I went to see the lecture-room of Fray Luis, a white-washed room, large, dark and square, with a vaulted ceiling. Narrow benches and narrow desks fill the whole space, and at the side is a long, boxed-off passage where, it appears, the spectators stood. Over the pulpit at the back is a wooden hood somewhat like a great extinguisher. It is from this pulpit that Fray Luis, according to the legend, in which, however, the learned declare there is no truth, gave that lecture the first words of which have carried his name down to posterity more firmly than any of his works. After four years in the prisons of the Inquisition he was acquitted and returned to Salamanca. He was received to the sound of drums and trumpets by a great concourse of gentle-men, professors at the University and students, who came out on to the road from Valladolid to meet him. After a due interval he gave his first lecture. A crowd collected to hear him. They expected him to attack his accusers and once more to speak in his own defence. He began with the words: 'As we were saying yesterday.'

While he was in prison he wrote his most celebrated work. It is called De los Nombres de Cristo. This book is in the form of a dialogue between three friends in the Augustinian order whom the heat of summer has brought to the house of the community on the Tormes a few miles from Salamanca. It was called La Flecha. The scene of the various conversations is in the garden of this and on a little island in the river. I thought I should like to see a spot so celebrated in Spanish letters and having inquired the way, set out; but after driving for some time I began to think I had lost it. Presently I met a fat young priest, with a round, red face and spectacles, who was strolling along the road reading his breviary. I stopped the car and asked him if he could direct me. He seemed glad to do so. He was a poor parish priest, in a shabby cassock discoloured by sun and rain, and he talked in a high-pitched voice. He was very polite and when he got into the car and then out again took off his hat, but when he put it on seemed very uncertain which was the front and which the back. He never stopped smoking cigarettes he deftly rolled himself.

After a while he put up his hand and we stopped. A

rough path led to the shady garden, surrounded by a
hedge of box, where the friar sat and chatted with his
friends. A brook ran by it, a tiny trickle of very clear
water, and beyond was an orchard. It was a quiet and
pleasant spot and the coolness was grateful in the heat
of the Castilian summer. The priest showed me this
place with a sort of proprietary air that I found very
delightful and then he did a singular thing. He began
to recite.

'Era por el mes de Junio, à las bueltas de la fiesta de
San Juan, al tiempo que en Salamanca comiençan à
cessar los estudios . . .'

It was the beginning of the book, and the liquid,
exquisitely balanced periods fell from his lips like music.
On his fat, red face was a look of rapture.

'What a memory!' I cried, when at last he stopped.

'I have read it so often. I often have long walks to
the farms in my parish, three and four and five leagues,
and it shortens the way if I repeat to myself my
favourite passages. No one ever wrote Spanish like
my Fray Luis.'

Then he said he would show me the island on which
Fray Luis used to walk and we returned to the high
road. This offered a wide prospect over the plain of
Castile. In the distance the hills were diaphanous. We
walked along the river, bordered with handsome, close-
growing poplars, till we came to a farm built on the
bank of the river, and here on a little terrace overlooking

the water a woman with a handkerchief over her head was busy sewing. She greeted the shabby young priest with affection and me with politeness and we passed through a mill on to the island. Beyond the mill-race the water seemed only just to flow. On the farther bank was a line of poplars and then the fields dry and brown after the harvest. A faint, pleasant breeze blew on the island, and here in a little circle of trees was a table where tradition says the friar sat and wrote. Now holiday-makers come on Sundays to picnic and the ground was strewn with old newspapers. The spot was exquisitely peaceful. The broad, placid river had a curious effect on one. One's mind was tranquil, but at the same time alert and buoyant.

But the recollection I brought away from the excursion was of this stolid peasant priest reciting line after line of that harmonious prose.

I have read the book from which he quoted, not every word of it, but a great deal. It consists of a series of homilies upon the appellations given to Jesus Christ in the scriptures, and I must admit I should have found it heavy going but for the charming descriptions with which the dialogues open, the digressions and illustrations, and the revelations here and there of the author's character. The reflections which are aroused in him by the subjects of his discourse do not seem to me of great subtlety. I should have thought them within the scope of any pious man who had an intimate acquaintance with theological literature.

To me there seems something extraordinarily modern about Luis de Leon. He was not all of a piece as so often appear the famous figures of the past. I do not suppose men then were any different from what they are now, but it looks as though to their contemporaries they seemed more homogeneous. Otherwise they could hardly have so often described them in terms of 'humours.' But Fray Luis was a contradictory creature in whom dwelt uneasily incongruous qualities and warring instincts. Pacheco, the father-in-law of Velasquez, has painted him in a few words: a little man, but well proportioned, with a big head covered with curly hair, a wide forehead, a round, rather than a long, swarthy face, and sparkling green eyes. He was vain and humble, arrogant and patient, sombre, peevish, bitter, loyal and chivalrous. He loathed fools and hypocrites. He was very tender to little children. He loved nature and truth. He was fearless. No matter what enmities he aroused he was always prepared to denounce tyranny; he would incur any danger to combat injustice. He was an ascetic, of great abstemiousness, and he seldom allowed himself the luxury of going to bed, so that the servitor who entered his cell in the morning found it as he had left it the night before. But he loved the fair things of life, the lovely, lulling sound of the Tormes flowing by La Flecha, the heavenly music of blind Salinas and the harmony and cadence of the Spanish tongue. He was quarrelsome, rude, violent, and he yearned above all else for peace. The cry for rest, rest from the turmoil of his thought, rest from the torment of the world, recurs in all his works. It gives his lovely lyrics a poignancy that pierces the artificiality of their Horatian manner. He sought for happiness and tranquillity of spirit, but his temperament made it impossible for him to achieve them. They count him among the mystics. He never experienced the supernatural blessings which solace those that pursue the mystic way. He never acquired that aloofness from the things of the world that characterises them. He had an anxious longing for a rapture his uneasy nature prevented him from ever enjoying. He was a mystic only in so far as he was a poet. He looked at those snowcapped mountains and yearned to explore their mysteries, but he was held back by the busy affairs of the city. I always think that the phrase of his, no se puede vivir sin amar, one cannot live without loving, had for him an intimate, tragic meaning. It was not just a commonplace.

Fray Luis had something of the universal capacity that we wonder at in certain figures of the Italian Renaissance. He was a mathematician, an astrologer and a jurist. Untaught, he acquired considerable proficiency as a painter. He was not only deeply versed in theological literature, but also in the classics, and their dreams of the Golden Age never ceased to haunt him.

He wrote some exquisite lyrics, after San Juan de la Cruz he is the best poet his country has produced, and I think all judges admit that nobody in Spain ever wrote prose so perfectly. Pen in hand Fray Luis was a scholar and a gentleman; he wrote with elegance, rather than with vigour. In La Perfecta Casada he quotes at length from Tertullian and even in the translation you can hardly fail to see how much more vivid, racy and virile was the African writer. But even a foreigner cannot but be sensible to the charm of Luis de Leon's liquid prose. It is as clear as the rivulet that runs through La Flecha. It is eloquent and at the same time colloquial; it is concise and yet abundant. It has a grave, playful music. To my cheerful mind the most attractive and diverting book of Fray Luis is The Perfect Wife. The reader, interested neither in theology nor in mysticism, can read it with entertainment. It offers sage counsel to a bride on her conduct in the various necessities of the married state. One cannot help feeling a certain amused astonishment at its curious mixture of simplicity, shrewdness and nobility. Incidentally it gives a pleasant glimpse of domestic life in the upper class and a hint here and there of circumstances which the conventional view of Spanish society would never have led you to suspect. Fray Luis was a Castilian gentleman of excellent family and his ideal of the good life was that of the landowner living on the produce of his estate. He does not seem to have considered the possibility that men might be born so unhappily as to have no broad acres to till. He had only scorn for such as engaged in commerce; it was not only disreputable, but gravely prejudicial to the soul's well-being. 'The life of the field,' he says, 'and the cultivation of one's inheritance is a school of innocence and truth because one learns from those with whom one works and talks. And as the earth renders faithfully what is entrusted to it, and in its unchangeableness is stable and downright, bountiful in its fruits and generous of its riches, liberal and productive to well-doing; so it seems to engender and to impress in the breasts of them that work it a peculiar goodness and a simplicity of temper such as are found with difficulty in men of other kinds. So it teaches sincerity, true and faithful dealing and keeps in remembrance the good old customs.'

The longest chapter is devoted to an attack, supported by abundant quotations from the classics and the fathers, on the unaccountable mania the women of his day had for dyeing their hair and painting their cheeks. (He thought, the good monk, that the beauty of a good woman resided not in the lineaments of her face, but in the secret virtues of her soul; and he was not sure that it became the perfect wife to be fair and lovely.) He admitted that not all women who painted had evil intentions. 'It is politeness to think so,' he remarks dryly. But if this mask on the face did not discover their bad desires, at all events it aroused those of their neighbours. This is how virtuous women should perform their toilet: 'Let them hold out their hands and receive in them water poured from a jar, which their servant will pour from the washing-stand, and let them put it to their faces, and take some of it in their mouths and wash their gums, and rub their fingers over their eyes and in their ears, and behind the ears also, and let them not desist till their whole face is clean; and after that, letting the water be, let them cleanse themselves with a rough towel, and so will they remain more beautiful than the sun.'

There is one chapter that is headed: 'How important it is that women should not talk much and that they should be peaceable and of a gentle disposition.' In this he has a phrase so modern that it makes one smile; he remarks that a 'foolish and chattering woman, as foolish women generally are, whatever other merits she has, is an intolerable business.' Further on he observes that the peculiarity of stupidity is that it is not aware of itself but contrariwise takes itself for wisdom. 'And whatever we do it will be the greatest difficulty to instil common sense (into persons of this sort), for that is something you learn ill if you do not learn it with your mother's milk. . . . And the best advice we can give to such women is to beg them to hold their tongues; since there are few wise women they should aim at there being many silent ones.' Before I leave this engaging work I should like to give an extract from the chapter entitled:

'On the obligation of married couples to love one another and to assist one another in their labours.' It is a quotation from St. Basil. 'The viper, the most ferocious animal among reptiles, assiduously goes out to espouse the sea-lamprey, and having arrived, whistles, as though to give the signal that he is there, and attract her from the sea so that he may take her in his marital embrace. The lamprey obeys and rejoins the poisonous and savage beast without fear. What do I say to this? What? That however harsh and of savage qualities the husband may be, it is necessary for the wife to put up with it and that she should not allow peace to be disturbed for any cause.'

That's talking, that is.

No one has ever thought even of beatifying Fray Luis de Leon. He never attained the peace that rewards the saints. By way of contrast I will give now a brief account of one whose way of life shows pre-eminently how mighty was the force that inspired these Spaniards. This is St. Peter of Alcantara and here is what St. Teresa says of him in her autobiography.

'How good an example has God lately taken from us in the blessed Father Peter of Alcantara. The world is not able to endure such perfection. They say that our health is more feeble and that times have changed. This holy man was in our own time; his spirit was mighty and so he held the world beneath his feet. And though men may go not naked nor make such harsh mortifications as he did, there are many things, as I have said on other occasions, whereby they may trample on the world, and the Lord teaches them when he sees that courage is there. And how great was that which God gave to this saint of whom I am speaking to enable him to perform for seven and forty years the harsh mortifications that are known to all. I want to say something about it for I know it is all true.

'He told me and another person from whom he kept little (me for the love he bore me, and this the Lord willed him to have in order to protect and encourage me at a time of great need, as I have said and will ever say), that for forty years, I think he said it was, he had slept only an hour and a half between day and night; and that this at the beginning was the most difficult mortification he performed, to conquer sleep; and in order to do it he always stood or knelt. When he slept it was sitting up, his head resting against a little piece of wood driven into the wall. He could not have lain down even if he had wanted to because his cell, as is well known, was only four and a half feet long. During all those years he never put on his hood, however hot was the sun, or whatever the rain, nor anything on his feet, nor garment save a habit of sackcloth, with nothing underneath, and this as tight as he could bear it, and a little cloak of the same stuff over it. He told me that in the great cold he took this off, and left the door and the little window of his cell open so that when he put on the cloak again and shut the door he might satisfy his body with the comfort of greater warmth. It was very usual for him to eat every third day. And he asked me why this astonished me, for it was very possible to anyone who accustomed himself to it. A companion of his told me that it happened to him to go a week without eating. This must have been when he was in prayer, for then he had great raptures and ecstasies of love for God, of which I was myself once a witness.

'In youth his poverty was extreme, and his mortification, for he told me that it had happened to him to live for three years in a house of his order without knowing a friar except by the sound of his voice; for he never raised his eyes; and so when he was obliged to go from place to place he did not know the way and had to follow the fathers. This happened on journeys. Women he never looked at and that for many years. He told me that now it was all the same to him whether he saw them or not; but he was very old when I came to know him, and his weakness was so great, he seemed to be made of nothing but the roots of trees. With all this holiness he was very affable, though of few words, unless you asked him questions. His answers were very delightful, for he had an excellent understanding. I should like to say much more, but I am afraid you will ask what business I have to write this. I have written it with misgiving. And so I will leave the matter only adding that he died as he had lived, preaching and admonishing his friars. When he saw his end approaching he said the psalm: *Laetatus sum in his quae dicta sunt mihi*, and kneeling down, died.'

No wonder they were able to conquer half the world, these Spaniards, when they could so terribly conquer themselves.

XII

I WISH it had been to my purpose to write an essay on mysticism. It is a fruitful subject. I have but tried to set down a few things about certain devout persons that might help me to some understanding of the religious spirit that was more than a background, that was the framework, in which the Spanish life of this particular period pursued its variegated activity. I do not suppose that at any time in the world's history religion entered so much into the common round of every day as in Spain just then. The main business of the Spaniard's life was his salvation. The picaroon heard mass on his way to commit one of his mean crimes and the pimp, the blackmailer, the hired bravo when he was wounded in a fray cried frantically for a priest to shrive him. Don Juan himself, the scoffer, when the statue's fiery grip fastened on him begged for a brief respite that he might make his peace with God. The Spaniards of the Golden Age looked upon the Catholic Church as the country of their souls; it inspired them indeed with the emotion made up of pride and affection, trust and nostalgia, which Dr. Johnson described as the last refuge of a scoundrel.

But by this time I thought I had gathered together sufficient material for my purpose. In the course of my reading I had collected a number of incidents to give movement to my narrative and I had on the brink of my consciousness a variety of personages who only awaited their call to take part in its action. Nothing remained for me but to sit down and start writing. Then a very unfortunate thing happened to me. Finding myself once in Cadiz I went to the picture gallery. It is on the first floor of an old palace, rather shabby, not at all extensive, and most of the pictures are by modern Spanish painters. They are deplorable. But in one room is a collection of pictures by Zurbaran which have been removed from the Carthusian monastery near Jerez. Zurbaran is not a painter for whom many people feel enthusiasm. You have to know him well, and study him, to realise how remarkable an artist he was. He had power, and that is a quality you seldom find in painters. But this is not the place to say much of him and my immediate business is only with these portraits. They purport to be portraits of various personages whose piety illustrated the Carthusian order; it seems probable that they are in fact portraits, and one would say speaking likenesses, of the monks who were in the monastery when Zurbaran went there to paint the pictures that were to adorn its walls. They are painted with the tightness that characterised him. Those white robes do not seem made of wool, but of a material as rigid as baize, and the folds have none of the yielding quality of stuff; they might be carved in wood. But the harshness, the stiffness, of the manner gives you rather a curious feeling. It may be repellent, but it does not leave you indifferent. There is something very impressive about this series of Carthusian saints and beatified monks. One, representing the Blessed John Houghton, strangely moved me. I could not but believe that it was an English monk and not a Spanish one that had been the model of this great-souled Englishman of whom his biographer says that he was shy in look, modest in manner, sweet in speech, chaste in body, humble of heart, amiable and beloved by all. There was here the well-bred refinement, the clear-cut, delicately beautiful features that you sometimes find in a certain sort of Englishman of gentle birth. The hair, the little of it that was left round the shaven skull, seemed to be of a reddish brown. For a moment I asked myself idly who was this unknown compatriot that had wandered so far from his native country to the monastery in Andalusia and, obedient to his Superior, sat to the painter for a portrait of another Englishman.

It was a face of great distinction, thin as though from long fasting, and with a tension that was restless and eager. On the cheeks was a hectic flush. The skin was darker than ivory, though with the warmly supple hue of ivory and paler than olive, yet with something of that colour's morbid delicacy. One wasted hand was

clasped to his breast and in the other he held a bleeding
heart. Round his neck, fastened by a knot, was the rope
of discipline.

I could not get the face out of my mind. Months
passed, a year, two years, and the character that
gradually acquired substance to undergo the adventures
and suffer the experiences for which I had made these
studies, took on the ascetic features, the thin, suffering,
eager and ecstatic look of that unknown monk. He had
the same spiritual air and his eyes in just the same way
were intent on an ineffable mystery. I thought nothing
of it; but when I came to close quarters with my subject
I saw that this was not the sort of man to do at all. In
the first place this was not a man of robust humour. I
suspected that before entering religion he had had some
sense of it, but of a thin, donnish kind that found a false
quantity very ridiculous and in his moments of abandon
led him to make witty quotations from Virgil. I could
see him smile dryly, and a trifle superciliously, I could
not imagine that he ever laughed out loud. I could
imagine that he was capable of love, but not of sen-
suality, and if he fell in love it would be tragically. I
could see him eating his heart out for some light woman
to whose worthlessness his idealism blinded him, or in
tortured silence for honour or God renouncing a
happiness that was his for the asking. I could not see
him tumbling a serving wench on a bed or deceiving
the jealous lover of a pretty actress. I thought it

possible that he would with pleasure converse with
Lope de Vega on the intricacies of versification, but he
would consider the drama no more than the entertainment of the vulgar. He would pass through the
student's life at Salamanca without communication
with any but a few serious and high-born gentlemen
and I think he would only despise the Horatian nostalgia
of the petulant Luis de Leon. If he read the picaresque
novels it would be as an idle pastime. He was not
curious to see for himself the life they described. He
left that to his lacqueys. With his exquisite manners he
kept the busy, bustling, sordid and picturesque world at
arm's length.

Such a person was not of the least use to me. I set
myself to think of another. I wanted someone gay,
intelligent but urbane, with a lively sense of humour,
religious of course, but with a spark of scepticism, eager
for adventure and interested in all the ideas he came
across, a man who could make himself at home in any
company, as much at his ease discussing the modern
drama with the poets as making merry with the players
or carousing with picaroons, a man who could tell a
good story, make love to a pretty woman, draw his
sword at a slight, hold his own in diplomatic intrigue
and yet hankered, wistful and reluctant, for the beauty
the mystics told of. I did not think there would be any
difficulty in fashioning a youth to suit my purpose. I
liked the idea of his having reddish hair and the ivory-

olive skin that sometimes goes with it. I gave him the thin face, the eager eyes, the clear-cut features that would correspond with his love of art and his interest in the things of the spirit. I did not want him too big and beefy, for that suggested a coarseness of disposition that was not in my idea of him; I wanted him to be elegant in appearance and well-proportioned, slender but strong, with the beautiful, long hands that El Greco would have been so charmed to paint. And when I had done with him I discovered to my dismay that I had described over again the white-robed Carthusian who sat for the portrait of the Blessed John Houghton. I began once more. The same thing happened to me; I left it for a while, I went back to it; it was no good; try as I would it was impossible for me to see him with any lineaments but those of that confounded monk. One might have supposed that an author could give a character any traits, physical and mental, that he chose. It is not so. The author does not create a character, at all events it is not his awareness that creates him; on the contrary he creates himself, it may be as in this case from a picture, it may be from the recollection of some one seen in the street or in past time known; and then his distinctive features grow round him, coming, I suppose, from the depths of the author's subconscious but without any impulse of his will. Once there the author can do nothing but accept him. He cannot, without making him unreal, change the colour of his hair or the shape of his mouth. The man is what he is because he is exactly so tall and he will do such and such a thing and feel such and such an emotion because he has just that look in his eyes. Pascal said that it would have changed the history of the world if Cleopatra's nose had been longer; he might have added that it would have changed too the plausible harmony which was her character. I was obliged to face the fact that the protagonist of the book I had in mind to write could be none other than this unknown monk. But this made it a book that I very well knew I could not write. It was not even a book that it much interested me to write. It would be somewhat excessively cultured, a trifle anæmic, and to me certainly of no particular significance. In fact I saw it as a kind of modern Marius the Epicurean with a setting in the Spain of the sixteenth century. That was not my cup of tea.

I struggled a little, but it availed me nothing. The hound of heaven pursued me. My character had killed my story. I resigned myself at last and made up my mind not to write my book after all. I was disappointed because I had worked at it desultorily for years and with application for three; I had read between two and three hundred books. I could only console myself by thinking that perhaps they had been of profit to me. The author cannot improve himself by a deliberate effort, for as I grow older I am more and more convinced that it is not he that writes but what they call his subconscious, and his aim must be to train and to enrich this in every way he can. This, I think, he can do by taking thought. There are some words of St. Teresa that can hardly fail to echo in the artist's heart: 'I am like one who hears a voice from afar off,' she says, ' but although hearing the voice cannot distinguish the words; for at times I do not understand what I say, yet it is the Lord's pleasure that it should be well said, and if at times I talk nonsense that is because it is natural to me to make a mess of everything.' I cannot believe that my long wandering through the Spanish country of to-day and through the spiritual country of the Golden Age, tedious as this sometimes was, has left me entirely as I was before. It has seemed to me that perhaps a reader here and there might be interested in the simple story of my journey.

But before taking my leave of him I should like to tell him one more thing. While I was pursuing these studies I read a great many narratives of travellers in Spain during the sixteenth and seventeenth centuries; I hoped from them to learn something of the manners and customs of the people and what the places looked like that the writers passed through. For the most part they are dull reading. We sigh now when we read the jokes of the facetious traveller who looks upon a journey into a strange country as an opportunity to exercise his wit and we yawn over the gushing word pictures of the artist in prose. It may be that in three hundred years they will have their interest. Alas, we shall all be long since dead. The travellers of the sixteenth century seem to have had no curiosity. Sometimes they sought to instruct and then gave a certain amount of information about the trade and manufactures of the places they visited. They seldom thought it worth while to note a picturesque detail. What was strange to them seemed on the whole unpleasant. I have referred two or three times to A Journey into Spain by van Aarssens. He is one of the most interesting. His description of Madrid is vigorous. He had a certain acid humour. But the greater part of his book is concerned with the intrigues of the Court, the political situation, and an account of various people of importance in their day; and much of it now is of no great moment. Most of the travellers confined themselves to recording the number of miles from stage to stage and to mentioning the names of the persons who treated them with civility. They were nearly always in a bad temper. And they had cause to be. In book after book the same complaints recur of the badness of the roads, the danger of brigands, the difficulties of supply and the verminous condition of the inns. Even St. Teresa, notwithstanding her passion to mortify the flesh, found these sometimes intolerable. Once, in a room with no window, the bed was so bad that she preferred to sleep on the floor.

Now among the books I read was one which had really nothing to do with me, for it was an account of a pilgrimage made to various holy places by an Armenian bishop at the end of the fifteenth century and this was a hundred years before the period with which I was concerned. But I saw the title in a bibliography and it excited my curiosity. It was Relation d'un Voyage fait en Europe. It was published in Paris in 1827 and the translation is by a Monsieur J. Saint Martin. It is a slim book, rather musty, its pages stained by time, and the French and the Armenian face one another. It begins with these words—I translate from the French:

'I, Martyr, but only by name, born at Arzendjan, and bishop, living in the hermitage of Saint Ghiragos at Norkiegh (the new village) had long wished to visit the tomb of the holy prince of the Apostles. When the time had come for me, unworthy though I was, to deserve this honour, which I never ceased to desire, without however ever having made known to anyone the intention in my heart, I went forth from my monastery on the twenty-ninth of October in the year 938 of the Armenian Era. Travelling by short stages, I arrived at Stamboul. There by the grace of God I found a ship on which I embarked with the deacon Verthanes.'

The date mentioned corresponds to 1489 of our era. It was on the third of August, 1492, that Christopher Columbus set sail from Palos to discover a new route to the Indies.

I think he must have been a remarkable man, Martyr, Bishop of Arzendjan. Arzendjan was a busy and populous city and Euphrates, the famous river, ran through it. It was in a plain, rich with orchards and vineyards, surrounded by hills in which dwelt wild tribes subjected to no authority. In the Euphrates, not far from the city, St. Gregory the Illuminator baptised the Armenian king and the nobles of his court; an event the results of which were very unfortunate for the Armenians and highly embarrassing to the Concert of Europe. The bishop made his way to Rome and here the Pope gave him a letter of recommendation which was of great service to him on his arduous journey. He made his way north and at Bâle he and his companion were arrested as spies. He makes no comment. On their release, following the course of the Rhine they reached Cologne where they saw the tombs of the Three Kings. When they got to Flanders, being unacquainted with the language, they had great difficulty in making themselves understood. For the same reason they found themselves in a quandary when they came to England, and he says nothing of it but that the English were fish-eaters. But reaching Paris, where he lodged at an inn, he cries: 'What man could describe the beauty of this city! It is a very great and splendid city.' That is farther than he goes often, for mostly he only tells how he went from place to place and what shrines he visited. He tells you nothing of the people he meets. It is the dryest reading possible and yet you read on because you have a sense of the man's indomitable courage. In Paris the deacon

Verthanes left him. He sought for another companion, but could, it appears, find no one willing to share the risks and hardships of the way. 'Putting my trust then in the prayers of St. James and in Almighty God I continued my journey in great affliction.' No dangers daunt him. He endures cold and hunger. Going on foot, by himself, a man no longer young, he accepts without a murmur whatsoever befalls him. When he arrives at a town he is entertained in a monastery, but if he finds himself in the open country he is prepared to sleep on the bare ground. He travelled through a multitude of towns, being received everywhere with great honour, and at St. Sebastian the host of the inn and his wife treated him with boundless charity. It is the only good that I have ever read of a Spanish inn-keeper. Two collections were made on his behalf, for whatever money he started with must have been long since spent. Of St. Sebastian he says, very surprisingly: 'I did not see a pretty face in this town.' And at last, very tired and weak, but sustained by the help of God, he came to the famous city where St. James had chosen his last resting place.

'I approached this tomb; I adored it my face to the earth, and I besought the remission of my sins, those of my father and mother, and those of my benefactors. At last I accomplished, with a great effusion of tears, what was the desire of my heart.'

Then he started on his homeward journey.

At last he arrived at a place that he calls Getharia, a port on the coast of Guipuzcoa. It was now 1494. He had been on the road for five years. It was but twelve months since Christopher Columbus had returned to Palos; he had found, not what he sought, but a new world. Now I go on with the bishop's narrative.

'I found in that place a great ship which they told me was of sixty tons burthen. I addressed myself to the priests to say that I should be taken in this ship: "I cannot go on foot any more," I said, "my strength is all gone." They were surprised that I could have come on foot from a country so far away. They went to see the captain of the ship: "this Armenian religious," they said to him, "begs you to take him in your ship: he has come from a far country and he is unable to return by land." They read him the Pope's letter; he listened to it and said: "I will take him in my ship; but tell him that I go to range the universal sea, that my ship carries no merchant, and that all the men who are in her are engaged in her service. As for us, we have made the sacrifice of our lives; we place our hope only in God, and we believe that whithersoever fortune carries us, God will save us. We go to rove the world and it is not possible for us to tell where the winds will carry us. But God knows. For the rest, if it is your wish also to come with us, it is very well; come in my ship, and do not concern yourself with bread, nor with food or drink. For whatever else you need, it is your business, these religious will see to it; since we have a soul, we will provide you with biscuit and all else that God has vouchsafed us." '

For sixty-eight days the intrepid bishop sailed the unknown seas. Contrary winds drove them hither and thither and they came at last to the town 'which is at the end of the world.' They had been so buffeted by violent storms and the great ship so shaken, they were obliged to make their way back to Cadiz for repairs. Here he left her and went on a pilgrimage to Santa Maria de Guadalupe. It was not till Lent in 1496 that he arrived once more in Rome. This is how he ends his narrative: 'I then went to Santa Maria where I took ship and I again endured such misfortunes that I would have preferred death rather than suffer so many dangers.'

But it is not for his own sake that I have written this of Martyr, Bishop of Arzendjan, though I do not think it is wasted time to consider for a little a good and a brave man. It is for the speech that the unknown captain of the ship made him when he asked for a passage, and I like to think that the Armenian bishop thought it a fine speech too, for in the course of his book it is the only one he reports. He mentions only and does not describe his meetings with sundry of the great. For my part I think it is as fine a speech as any that Thucydides gave to the famous men of Greece whose history he wrote. I suppose no one will ever

know the name of this sea-captain, who, putting his
trust in God, in a craft we know how frail, set out
to sail the universal sea. His words have the heroic
ring. I like to think that Bishop Martyr, 'by name
only,' recognised in him a kindred soul. He too,
the unknown captain, was a dedicated priest, but
to high adventure, and he too had a fearless heart.

And if I am not mistaken here is the secret of the
greatness that was Spain. In Spain it is men that
are the poems, the pictures and the buildings. Men
are its philosophies. They lived, these Spaniards
of the Golden Age; they felt and did; they did not
think. Life was what they sought and found, life
in its turmoil, its fervour and its variety. Passion
was the seed that brought them forth and passion
was the flower they bore. But passion alone cannot
give rise to a great art. In the arts the Spaniards invented nothing. They did little in any of those they
practised, but give a local colour to a virtuosity they
borrowed from abroad. Their literature, as I have
ventured to remark, was not of the highest rank;
they were taught to paint by foreign masters, but,
inapt pupils, gave birth to one painter only of the
very first class; they owed their architecture to the
Moors, the French and the Italians, and the works
themselves produced were best when they departed
least from their patterns. Their preëminence was
great, but it lay in another direction: it was a pre-

ëminence of character. In this I think they have been surpassed by none and equalled only by the ancient Romans. It looks as though all the energy, all the originality, of this vigorous race had been disposed to one end and one end only, the creation of man. It is not in art that they excelled, they excelled in what is greater than art—in man. But it is thought that has the last word.

THE END